Coin World

● THE WEEKLY NEWSPAPER OF THE ENTIRE NUMISMATIC FIELD ●

Beginner's Guide
to
Collecting Coins
and
Paper Money

By the
Editors of
Coin World

Written by
Paul Gilkes
Coin World Staff Writer

Coin World staff also contributing to this book:
Beth Deisher, William T. Gibbs, P. Bradley Reed

A SIGNET BOOK

NEW AMERICAN LIBRARY
A DIVISION OF PENGUIN BOOKS USA INC.

SIGNET TRADEMARK REG. U.S. PAT. OFF. AND FOREIGN COUNTRIES
REGISTERED TRADEMARK—MARCA REGISTRADA
HECHO EN DRESDEN, TN, U.S.A.

SIGNET, SIGNET CLASSIC, MENTOR, ONYX, PLUME, MERIDIAN
and NAL BOOKS are published by New American Library, a division of
Penguin Books USA Inc., 1633 Broadway, New York, New York 10019

First Printing, March, 1990

1 2 3 4 5 6 7 8 9

PRINTED IN THE UNITED STATES OF AMERICA

Contents

Getting started

1

Question: How many sides does a coin have?

Answer: Would you be surprised that the answer is "three"?

Everyone recognizes the "heads and tails" of a coin, what coin collectors refer to as **"obverse** and **reverse."** The third side is the **edge.** The edge of a coin may have its own design. It can be plain, like a cent, or reeded, like a dime, or have any variation of lettering or designs.

Just as there are more sides to a coin than you might expect, so are there more sides to the hobby of collecting money than may be obvious at first glance.

Coin collecting is just one small part of the broader field of **numismatics** (pronounced noo-miz-ma-ticks) — the science, study or collecting of coins, tokens, medals, orders and decorations, paper money, primitive money and related items.

Under the broader umbrella of numismatics is crowded every medium of exchange used by man for more than 2,600 years; whether it be an animal's tooth, a bronze necklace, official coinage issues in various metals, or paper currency, from nations around the world.

People also collect unofficial money substitutes, such as **tokens**, which are accepted for use in commerce and trade in exchange for goods and services.

The umbrella of numismatics also covers items produced in a manner similar to the production of money. **Medals**, produced in a wide range of materials in a variety of shapes and designs, may picture subjects to honor a nation's statesmen, to commemorate a sports event, or provide for the engraver an outlet for creating original designs. Many people collect medals designed or engraved by artists who also design coins.

A similar range of fields is open to collectors of paper money. Collectibles range from official issues of governments, to special-use issues such as military scrip or emergency money, to privately issued notes. Many paper money collectors also collect **souvenir cards** or **vignettes** which are produced in a manner similar to the

Money has taken many odd and curious forms.

manufacture of paper money, or which may depict the artistry of paper money engravers.

And under the umbrella of numismatics is the very popular field of collecting error coins and paper money. Much of the appeal of error coins and notes is in their curiosity. But much can be learned about the manufacturing process by examining certain error pieces. More will be explained about the manufacturing process in a later section.

Collecting money and related items can appeal to people of any social or economic background.

There are almost as many reasons for collecting money as there are collectors. To some, their collections are primarily financial investments. Most collectors, however, while keenly aware of the financial worth of their collections, have additional motives for collecting.

Coins and other numismatic items give us a valuable perspective on the cultures that create and use them. From a historical point of view, coins depict statesmen, athletes, scientists, and even mythological characters. Even the denominations of coins, the metals used in producing them, and the methods by which they are produced convey a great deal of historical information.

Some coins are "souvenirs" of ancient times that we can hold in our hands. By collecting and studying them, we can learn what ancient people considered valuable, what symbols or ideals were important to them, and the sophistication of

THE TERM "EXONUMIA" refers to collectible items that are related to money, either by function, method of production or other means.

Ancient coins such as these tell us much about their makers.

their artists. In many cases, portraits engraved on coins are the only remaining images of the ceasars, emperors and kings of lands that now are little more than legend.

Paper money, too, is crowded with information about its people. Look at a note from a foreign land. You can get a feeling for the language, the artistic style, the cultural symbols of people you may never meet face to face. What do you think people in other countries can learn about us from looking at our money?

Look through the money in your pocket or purse. Have you ever wondered how it is made? Who decides what "pictures" or designs appear on our money? How did the likenesses of Presidents Lincoln, Washington, Jefferson, Roosevelt and Kennedy come to be on the coins we use today? Who created these likenesses? What is the purpose of the detailed engraving on our paper money? What is the meaning of the eye above the pyramid on the back of a dollar bill?

When you start asking yourself questions like these, and when you have the proper tools to find the answers, then you are well on your way toward graduating from mere accumulator of interesting items to becoming a true numismatist.

All these approaches to coin collecting and more are reflected in a rich tradition of numismatic literature. Entire libraries exist of thousands of books and other publications devoted to numismatics. Many collectors find as much enjoyment browsing through numismatic libraries as in collecting. At the same time, you need not be overwhelmed by this mass of learning. A few well-chosen reference works will provide the basic information needed for well-informed collecting. And having the book in hand can make a world of difference in the development of your collecting habits. A famous New York numismatist, Aaron Feldman, once said, "Buy the book before the coin." It makes sense.

SOME PEOPLE collect books as well as coins. They are called "bibliophiles."

Who was the first coin collector? No one really knows. Once considered a hobby for the wealthy and powerful, coin collecting has developed into a popular pastime for people in all walks of life.

You will certainly find it worthwhile to join a local coin club in your area where coin collectors with varied collecting interests can share their knowledge in, and enjoyment of, their specialized areas of collecting. Joining a coin club can provide you with information about other areas of material to collect that you may never have previously considered. If there isn't a coin club in your area, you may want to start one.

Your own interests and curiosity will guide you in what you decide to collect. You may want to concentrate on collecting **obsolete paper money** issued by banks that once thrived in the area in which you live. You may want to collect sports medals because you like sports. At least one collector we know collects transportation tokens because his grandfather worked as a train engineer.

The amount of money and time you spend on coin collecting depends not only on the area in which you want to specialize, but on how deeply you want to be involved. And as you become more involved, you will find you share similar interests with like-minded collectors.

For those who don't have money to burn, it would be unwise to spend a fortune trying to assemble a set of United States gold coins. If money is limited, you may want to start out conservatively by going to your local bank and buying $5 worth of Lincoln cents and trying to put together a set of dates and Mint marks.

MINT MARKS can be letters, numbers or symbols. They may appear on either side of a coin, and identify the Mint at which the coin was struck.

Coins can be collected according to date and the Mint mark, and can be placed in various kinds of coin folders available on the market today.

This method, followed by many beginning collectors, can provide you with hours of collecting enjoyment as you assemble, without too much trouble, a set of Lincoln cents with Lincoln Memorial reverse.

You may also find some "Wheat Ear" reverse issues the same way. The Lincoln Memorial reverse refers to the Lincoln Memorial pictured on the "tails" side of the cent from 1959 until the present. A **Wheat**

Lincoln got a new reverse in 1959, his 150th birthday.

Ear cent or "Wheatie" refers to the ears of wheat pictured on the reverse of the Lincoln cent from its introduction in 1909 until 1959, when it was replaced by the Lincoln Memorial reverse.

Many collectors recall the days when rare and scarce silver coins (dated before 1965 when copper-nickel clad coinage was first struck) could be found in pocket change. While **clad coins** — those made of a base metal such as copper and layered with a more valuable metal — have not generated as much fervor as their silver ancestors, it would be quite an accomplishment if you could assemble a complete set of perfectly struck dimes, quarter dollars and half dollars, from 1965 to date.

The most dedicated collector usually won't spend more for a particular issue than he expects to get back when he sells his collection. Even though certain series have experienced ups and downs in recent years, collections have continued to appreciate in value as time passes, and collectors have enjoyed the results, regardless of the motives for assembling their collections in the first place.

Although these collecting suggestions offer you little more financial reward than the face value of the coins being saved, they can provide valuable learning experiences for the beginning collector.

While hands-on experience is important and helpful, buying that first reference book covering your collecting interests is just as important. Research not only provides you with knowledge of world history, but also with the art and technology that goes into producing a specific numismatic item.

As with the collector, the investor must do more than just acquaint himself with the coins he plans to buy. He may have to learn much more to become familiar with how well the coins he plans to purchase have performed in the marketplace so he can maximize his investment. Nowadays, the investor and collector are often one.

A GOOD WAY to obtain foreign money is to ask friends who travel to bring some back for you.

Once you've had your collecting appetite whetted, where do you go to have your collecting interests satisfied?

Earlier, we suggested going to your local bank and buying $5 worth of Lincoln cents to begin assembling a collection. We also talked about the days, less than 25 years ago, when silver coins were readily available in circulation.

What if your interests lie in those silver coins, in early copper coins, world coins or paper money? Where are those kinds of numismatic collectibles found?

The number of places where you can buy coins and other numismatic items to start building your collection is endless. Possibilities include buying and trading with members at your local coin club; your local coin shop; mail order from advertisements in numismatic publications; mail-bid and public auctions; electronic teletypewriter trading and auctions; local coin shows and major coin conventions; professional numismatists; and government Mints.

You may also find success at estate auctions, and sometimes even at flea markets.

The key to successful coin collecting is knowledge. Know what you are looking for and what you are willing to pay.

Let's start with your local coin club. Your local coin club provides members the opportunity for trading and selling duplicate items from their collection. Clubs often hold monthly auctions whereby members sell coins and other numismatic items they no longer want because either they have duplicates, they've upgraded the item they want to sell with a better example for their own collection, or their collecting tastes have changed.

Often, each item put into these auctions costs only a few dollars, allowing everyone an inexpensive chance to obtain something new to add to their collection or to start a new collection. Such auctions are also a good means of gaining the interest of young collectors.

Your local coin dealer can also be very helpful. The dealer often has expertise in more than one area of numismatics, and can provide collecting tips. In addition to coins and other numismatic material, coin shops usually offer coin collecting reference books, coin holders, and other related accessories to make assemblage of a

IT MAY BE EASIER to buy coins than it is to sell them. Ask your dealer about his purchasing policies.

collection more organized, yet highly enjoyable.

Larger department stores in major cities may also have a professionally staffed numismatic department.

Some coin dealers participate in one or more electronic trading networks which allow the dealer to access, by computer or teletypewriter, coins being offered by other dealers. These networks also provide you, the collector or investor, with another means of locating the specific coin or coins you want, in the condition you want, at a price you're willing to pay.

Coin World, along with other numismatic newspapers and magazines, offers classified advertisements of numismatic material offered for sale through the mail. The classifieds are broken down into various collecting categories, from Lincoln cents to gold double eagles, from scarce and rare issues to common date offerings, Proof and Uncirculated Mint sets, paper money, and tokens and medals, among others.

BESIDES BEING a good place to find coins for sale, hobby publications can keep you informed of developments that could affect your collection.

You will also usually find, either in the classifieds or larger display ads, coins and other material offered for sale through electronic teletypewriter and computer trading, mail-bid, and public auctions. Dealers and individuals with computer or teletypewriter access to the subscribed services can do their trading, buying and selling without leaving their home or business.

Some auctions are also conducted by computer access.

Bidding by mail and public auctions can be offered separately, but sometimes together. Coin companies usually print a list of the material they will be offering — either by mail-bid, public auction, or both, with appropriate deadlines for the mail-bid option — in various numismatic publications or in fliers sent directly to regular customers.

These listings generally include the coin company's description of the coin or other items, the grade or condition of the item based on the company's assessment, and sometimes an estimated selling price or minimum bid price.

On sales that are strictly mail-bid, bidders send in a list of the coins they are bidding on and the price they want to pay. If yours is the highest bid on a particular coin, you have the "won" the right to buy that particular coin for the winning bid price.

However, read the guidelines and conditions for bidding and buying. Most dealers print their guidelines with the list of material offered. Some add a buyer's fee, often 10 percent of the winning bid, to the total purchase price as their commission. Some have buy-back policies in case you're not satisfied or think the item is not as described. Carefully read the conditions for bidding.

The larger coin auction companies not only advertise in various coin newspapers and periodicals, but also publish large, descriptive and extensively-illustrated catalogs of all the material being put on the auction block. The catalogs can be purchased from the various companies and are usually sent free to regular customers. The catalogs also list dates and lo-

IF AN AUCTION LOT has a "reserve bid," that means it may be withdrawn from the auction if the bidding does not go high enough.

cations of the actual public auction as well as those for viewing the items, or lots being offered.

Public viewing of the lots gives you, the potential bidder, the opportunity to look over the material to see if the material as described in the catalog meets your requirements. The auctions are then run like any other auction you may have attended. The lot goes to the highest bidder, and again, a buyer's fee is usually added to the **"hammer price"** or winning bid.

Some sales combine mail bidding with the public auction. Mail bidders compete with the public, or floor bidders, for the various auction lots. In most instances, the winning bid "goes to the floor" because by being in attendance you can experience the excitement of bidding, plus have the advantage of knowing what the mail bids are.

Some sales allow a mail bidder to register a preferred bid but also include a maximum price he is willing to pay. In this case, the bidder trusts the auctioneer to increase the bid up to the approved level, if necessary, so that the bidder may win the lot.

Some mail-bid sales allow you to bid on many lots, but specify a maximum total amount you wish to spend. Some mail-bid sales will also reduce the winning bid to a percentage above the second-highest bid. These are encouragements to bid boldly on lots you may want, but if someone else also bids high on the same lot, you may end up paying more than you bargained for! You can see why it is important to read and understand the rules for each mail-bid sale.

IF AN AUCTION LOT is available for inspection before the auction, you probably will not be able to return it if you are unsatisfied — know what you are buying!

Estate auctions and flea markets may also offer numismatic material. However, flea markets are not often staffed by professional numismatists and the material offered at estate auctions may not have been examined by a professional numismatist.

While estate auctions and flea markets can give you immediate access to numismatic material, be sure to examine the items carefully. Coins and related items sold at estate auctions and flea markets can be vastly over-priced. In some cases, you may find yourself getting a bargain. Again, knowledge is important.

Local coin shows and major coin conventions provide an arena for you to make contacts with coin dealers from your area or from around the country. The dealers may specialize in U.S. coins, paper money, gold and silver bullion, tokens, world coins, or offer a wide range of numismatic items.

The **bourse**, or sales floor of the coin

The coin show bourse has material for every collector.

show or convention, whether it's a 20-table show or a major convention of 150 or more tables, is the best place to start building your collection. You can even do a little dealing yourself.

The contacts you make on the bourse, whether coin dealers or other collectors, add to your knowledge of the hobby. You may want to look for dealers on the bourse who specialize in your area of collecting and who can help you select the coins you want for your collection and locate the hard-to-find pieces.

Many dealers are willing to take the time to talk with you, sharing their knowledge of a particular coin issue and offering collecting tips. Remember, most dealers on the bourse started out just like you, a beginning collector, before jumping into numismatics as a business.

Depending on your collecting habits, you may also want to consider "the source": government Mints or Treasuries.

The United States Mint is the arm of the Treasury Department responsible for manufacturing U.S. coins. Of course, its primary function is to produce coins for everyday circulation. But it also finds time to produce special pieces for collectors.

ONE ADVANTAGE to being on the U.S. Mint's mailing list is that you may receive pre-issue discount offers for some programs.

When directed by the United States Congress, the Mint offers limited-edition commemorative coins and medals in various metals and in a wide range of prices, from a few dollars to several hundred dollars each. Recent **commemorative coins** have commemorated the 1989 Bicentennial of the Congress and the 1988 Olympic Games. It has been the recent practice of Congress to attach a **surcharge** to the price of these commemoratives,

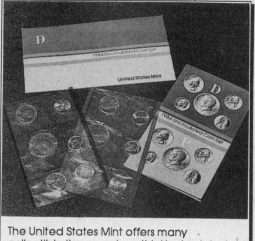

The United States Mint offers many collectible items, such as this Uncirculated Mint set.

which is paid to a worthy organization, such as the United States Olympic Committee for the Olympic commemorative program, or channeled directly to the United States Treasury.

From time to time, Congress awards gold medals to deserving individuals, and sometimes authorizes the Mint to sell bronze duplicates to the public. Less often, the Mint is authorized to strike medals to be sold by another organization, such as is the case with the Young Astronauts Council.

The Mint also manufactures and sells Uncirculated Mint sets and Proof sets to collectors. An **Uncirculated Mint set** is an official set containing one coin of each currently produced denomination from each of the Mints in operation. The coins are carefully handled and packaged.

Either directly through the mail or through official distributors, collectors can buy foreign material from the source.

In a **Proof set,** the coins are specially manufactured from cleaned and polished planchets, or blanks, using chrome-plated dies on special low-speed, multiple-strike presses. Proof coin manufacturing is very specialized. Most of the Proof coins currently produced by the United States Mint are produced by a single facility — the San Francisco Mint. And almost all of the coining capacity of the San Francisco Mint is devoted to Proof coin prduction.

The government Mints of Canada and Great Britain produce much of the world's coins, including coins specially produced for collectors. A coin issued for, say, the Bahamas was probably produced by the British Royal Mint in Llantrissant, Wales.

You may wish to receive regular mailings about coins available from various government Mints. Because so many nations do not produce their own coins, just a few mailing lists will allow you to watch for coins of many nations. Here are some starting points:

U.S. Mint, Customer Service
10001 Aerospace Road
Lanham, Md. 20706.

Royal Canadian Mint
P.O. Box 457, Station A
Ottawa, Ontario K1N 8V5 Canada

British Royal Mint
c/o Barclay's Bank of New York N.A.
P.O. Box 2570
New York, N.Y. 10163.

If your interest is in world coins or paper money, and you want to know how to write for information, *Coin World* maintains a list of sources. Write and specify the country or countries you are interested in to:

Coin World
How to Order Foreign Coins
P.O. Box 150
Sidney, Ohio 45365

Paper money collectors can also receive information from the source. To get on the mailing list of The Bureau of Engraving and Printing, the branch of the Treasury Department that prints stamps, paper money, souvenir cards and other paper numismatic items, write:

Office of External Affairs
Room 533M
Bureau of Engraving and Printing
14th and C Streets, SW
Washington, D.C. 20228

The American Bank Note Co. prints paper money for many countries. It also produces printed items specially made for collectors. Write to:

American Bank Note Co.
20 N. Airmont Road
Suffern, N.Y. 10901

If you don't have time to do the searching, but have the money, you may want to consider employing the services of a professional numismatist. Keep in mind that you're paying for the numismatist's expertise and time. The professional numismatist will, for a fee, assemble a collection according to your specifications.

As your agent, the professional numismatist will travel to coin shops, shows and conventions, look at hundreds of coins, and check the teletypewriter and computer coin-trading networks in search of those coins you want.

As you can see, there are a multitude of sources of numismatic material to start or add to your collection. Pick the ones that best suit you.

Origins of money

Before the advent of money in the form of coins, and later notes, transactions were accomplished through simple **barter**. Anything of value could be traded for something else of value. Work could be exchanged for food, food could be traded for clothing, clothing could be swapped for blankets.

Clearly prehistoric humans survived, and in some instances thrived, without money. But the advantages of a common "currency" are so strong that societies have made use of all sorts of things to serve the purpose — various metals, stones, tobacco, shells, even woodpecker scalps. In parts of Europe at the close of World War II, when many local economies had collapsed, cigarettes took on the function of money for a brief period.

The advantage of a commonly acceptable currency is one of convenience. In a simple barter system, a farmer who owns excess grain but needs baskets must find a basketweaver who needs grain. Then the farmer trades a portion of his grain for some of the basketweaver's wares.

In a complex barter system, the farmer could trade his grain for furs, then trade the furs for baskets. Money is an outgrowth of complex bartering. Instead of finding a commodity to trade, the farmer could sell his grain for cash, then pay the basketweaver cash for baskets. That way, if the basketweaver had no need of grain or of furs, he would still have an incentive to trade with the farmer — baskets for money.

EXPLORER MARCO POLO in his travels to China found salt cakes being used as money.

When the basketweaver has a need for some commodity, he can then take the cash he got from the farmer to buy whatever he needs.

As money is passed from hand to hand, it is said to **circulate.** We are so familiar with a cash economy that we find it difficult to imagine life without money. But try to picture modern life in a barter economy. For instance, if you needed a pair of shoes, you would have to seek out a shoemaker who has need of some service or product you could provide. You would haggle about how many hours of floor-sweeping it would take for him to provide you with a pair of shoes.

How many steps would it take for you to trade labor for the materials to manufacture, say, a bicycle? Money makes complex economies possible.

Designs on coins may be traced back to ancient times, in the period where lumps of metal were being transformed into coinage as we recognize it today. Small pieces of valuable metals, such as gold, silver or copper, were being traded in complex barter systems. They were traded by weight. The shekel, for instance, is recognized today as a denomination of money. But in ancient times, "shekel" was a specified weight of silver.

As trade came more and more to cross cultural bounds, the purity of the metals came to be questioned. If one culture's little gold lumps had more pure gold than another culture's little gold lumps, then the first's were more valuable for the same weight. Some money issuers began stamping a symbol of the culture as an assurance of the quality of the little gold lumps. These symbols grew into fully developed designs, and coinage as we know it was born.

Money systems almost always become **debased**. That means that over time, their **face value** exceeds their **intrinsic value**, or the value of the metal that makes up the coin. The coins of the United States are the sizes they are because at one time their intrinsic metal value was roughly equal to their face value. Quarters and dimes were made of silver; cents were made of copper. In the history of United States coinage, you will find many sizes of coins, almost always be-

Both coins have a face value of 1 cent, but the older coin is three times heavier, reflecting a change in a currency's purchasing power.

Silver certificates were once redeemable for silver coin.

ginning large and becoming smaller and lighter for the same face value.

Modern coins of the United States are extremely debased. The value of the copper and nickel in an Anthony dollar, Kennedy half dollar or Washington quarter is about 3 cents, far below their face values. Cents are now composed of a light plating of copper over a core of zinc. The metal value of a cent is far less than 1 cent.

Debasement is **inflationary**. Inflation means it takes more money to buy the same thing. Older readers will remember when gasoline was less than 30 cents per gallon. Younger readers will be amazed (and amused) to learn the seemingly small wages earned by their grandfathers.

Paper money developed with the banking industry. Banks as safe depositories for coinage or precious metals began issuing slips of paper testifying that a certain amount of money was being held.

Traders found that it was very convenient to merely trade the slips of paper, rather than go to the bank and withdraw the actual metal.

In the United States, **silver certificates** promising to pay the bearer in silver coin from the U.S. Treasury were issued as late as 1963. While still legal tender, they may no longer be redeemed for silver coin.

Paper money not backed by physical reserves of coinage or precious metal, or **specie**, is called **fiat** currency. "Fiat" comes from a Latin term meaning "let it be done." In other words, fiat money is worth something simply because the government says it is, not because it represents any actual store of wealth.

The concept of **legal tender** is one that many collectors will come across. It is sometimes misunderstood, and is sometimes abused or misused. Basically, legal tender is officially recognized money. In other words, a ruling body has decreed that certain kinds of money are acceptable, others are not.

Legal tender status has become especially fuzzy recently with the advent of the **legal tender bullion coin**. These are coins pro-

Legal tender has an official OK.

duced under authority of a government and intended to be purchased at their intrinsic metal value for investment purposes. Many, however, have a face value well below their actual metal value, entirely opposite of debased coinage. Where a Washington quarter may have 3 cents worth of metal but a face value of 25 cents,

INVESTORS USE the face value of legal tender bullion coins as a hedge; if the price of the precious metal drops dramatically, the coin would still be worth its face value.

an American Eagle gold bullion coin has $350 worth of metal but only $50 face value. Of course, no one actually expects bullion coins to circulate at their face values, but their legal tender status means they *could.*

The problem becomes even fuzzier with Proof legal tender bullion coins. These are coins with a face value, but not intended either for circulation or for investment, but rather for collectors.

Also, commemorative coins are given face values and legal tender status, even though they are not intended for use as money, but as collectibles.

It seems that collectors of commemorative coins and investors in bullion coins like the assurances of legal tender status. Legal tender coins are viewed as "better" or more legitimate than non-legal tender coins or medals.

Coinage in America

The history of American coinage predates Independence, going back to the mid 1600s and the production of the Massachusetts silver New England, Willow, Oak and Pine Tree coins. The Colonial coins of Massachusetts and privately issued copper tokens were joined in circulation by a bewildering mass of foreign gold, silver and copper pieces, notably Spain's silver reales (pronounced "ree-AH-les").

The popular Spanish silver **8 reales**, the "piece of eight," was the model for the U.S. dollar. A real was referred to as a **"bit,"** or 12-1/2 cents — thus giving rise to the present-day cheer "two bits, four bits, six bits, a dollar . . ."

The various states — most notably New Jersey, Massachusetts and Connecticut — issued copper coins in quantity after Independence. (Vermont issued its coinage as an independent republic before it became a state.)

In 1787, Congress authorized the first official U.S. coinage, the copper **Fugio cents**. These privately-struck pieces are named for their design of a sundial with Latin motto meaning "I Fly," urging thrifty use of time. Some numismatists credit Benjamin Franklin with at least the idea for the Fugio cent design.

The new Philadelphia Mint ceremonially struck its first silver coin, the **half disme** (pronounced "deem"), in 1792. Coinage for general circulation began the next year with copper half cents and large cents, which continued until 1857.

Though privately struck, the Fugio cents of 1787 are considered the first coins of the new United States government. The 13 linked rings on the reverse represent the original 13 states.

A variety of precious and non-precious metals have been used in minting U.S. coins since circulating coinage began. Silver was used in circulating coinage until 1965 when **clad** coins, those made by bonding one metal to another, were introduced.

Gold coins were issued until 1933, when the financial crisis of the Great Depression resulted in all gold coinage being stopped by presidential order.

Silver and gold are now used by the United States Mint only for minting commemorative coins and legal tender bullion coins.

Manufacturing coins

The first coins were crudely-struck lumps of hot metal, usually off-center and often split. A lump of metal would be placed onto an anvil and struck with a hammer. If dies were used, the designs of the dies would be transferred to the coin. Because of the irregularity of the hand-hammering process, most early coins are off center, and many are split around the outside. They don't have well-defined edges that we would recognize as part of modern coinage.

Some early coins were cast in molds. A form is constructed and hot metal poured in. When the mold is broken open, coins are made. Many artists use variations of this process to create art medals today.

The **screw press** improved the consistency of coin production. With a screw press, a planchet is placed onto the lower die (still technically called the **"anvil die,"** from the days of hammered coinage), and a weighted bar is turned, causing a screw to drive the **"hammer die"** into the coin metal. A hand-operated screw press re-

STEAM POWER was installed at the Philadelphia Mint in 1816, but the first steam-powered coining presses were not introduced until 1836.

This hand-operated screw press is on display at the Philadelphia Mint.

quires a person to set the planchets and remove the struck coins, and one or two people to turn the screw. Still, it dramatically increased production over the hand-hammered method.

With the Industrial Revolution came powered presses. Steam power eventually replaced man- or horse-power. Coin production today, while much, much faster with modern hydraulics and electronic controls, nevertheless bears amazing similarity to early machine production.

Modern U.S. coins are produced in factories, called Mints, owned and operated by the federal government. Mints are located in Philadelphia, Pa.; Denver, Colo.; San Francisco, Calif.; and West Point, N.Y.

Smaller nations may employ a government Mint or private mint in another country to produce their coins.

There are many methods of producing coins in use around the world. But

Planchets are punched from strip.

there are some general similarities of coin production. For our purposes, we will use the methods of the United States Mint as our example.

Coins begin as metallic ores, which are **assayed** (checked for the content of a specific metal or metals), refined, melted and formed into huge slabs of coinage alloy (mixture of more than one metal). The slabs are then passed through a series of rolling mills and are rolled flat to a specified thickness, at which point they are referred to as **"strip."**

Dime, quarter dollar and half dollar strip requires another step in which outer layers of copper-nickel are bonded to an inner core of pure copper. The coinage strip is trimmed and cleaned, then shipped to the Mint or to a private contractor for the production of planchets, also known as blanks.

To produce **planchets**, coinage strip is fed into heavy-duty punching machinery, which consists of a bank of metal punches and a lower steel bedplate full of holes aligned with the punches. The metal punches ram through the strip, punching out planchets on each downward cycle. Planchets are slightly larger than finished coins, and have rough edges, or burrs, because of the shearing action of the punches. These rough edges are smoothed down during succeeding preparation steps.

Since 1982, U.S. cent planchets have required another production step because the planchet consists chiefly of zinc instead of copper. The zinc-alloy planchets are given a thin plating of pure copper to resemble pre-1982 brass cents.

The planchets are passed over sorting screens, called **riddlers**, designed to

Seen from above, cent planchets are sorted by screens.

eliminate any undersized, non-round or otherwise defective blanks from getting into the coinage presses. The rejected planchets are melted for re-use.

During the finish rolling and blanking press operations, the planchets have been hardened and must now be softened. To accomplish this, the sorted planchets are sent to an annealing furnace. During this **annealing**, or softening process, the planchets are passed through a cylinder with spiral grooves in its walls. The planchets are forced from one end of the cylinder to the other by the spirals as the cylinder turns. As the planchets travel through the cylinder, they are heated to approximately 1400 degrees Fahrenheit, changing their crystal structure to a softer state. By placing the softened planchets immediately into a water-quench bath, the planchets can be "frozen" into that state. This softening process reduces the striking pressure necessary to produce well-struck coins, thereby prolonging the life of the coining dies.

The heat of the annealing furnace discolors the planchets, which are chemically cleaned and dried by hot air. After being cleaned and dried, the planchets go through **the upsetting mill**

The upsetting mill forms a rim on planchets.

— a rotating grooved wheel inside a fixed grooved "shoe" which places a raised rim on each planchet. The distance between the grooves in the wheel and the grooves in the shoe lessens as the planchet travels along the grooved path, squeezing the planchet and slightly reducing its diameter and creating a raised **rim**.

The rim readies the striking of the coin by sizing and shaping the planchet for better feed into the press, and the process hardens the edge to prevent metal from escaping between the parts of the coining press.

To become a coin, each planchet is struck between a pair of **dies**, or hardened metal punches, bearing the same image that will appear on the coin, only reversed and incused (recessed). The design on each die is a mirror-image of what will appear on the coin.

Actually, the creation of a new coin begins long before the steps outlined above. Once a coin design has been approved it is sculptured in modeling wax three to twelve times the intended size of the coin, and negative and positive plasticene (synthetic modeling clay) models are made from the sculpture.

At each step, details are retouched to preserve the integrity of the design. The positive-image epoxy model is placed on a reduction engraving machine, which cuts the design into a piece of steel, creating a positive **master hub** the same size as the finished coin.

The master hub is heat-treated to harden it, and then used to create a number of **master dies**. The images on the master dies are backwards and incused — they

CIRCULATING COINS are usually struck only once, but some Proof coins and bullion coins are struck two or three times to sharpen the design details.

look like inside-out coins. From these master dies, many **working hubs** are produced using the same process, and from each working hub are produced many **working dies**. The working dies are the actual dies used to strike coins.

Die pairs, or a matched obverse and reverse, are set into the **coining presses**. Some coining presses use just one die pair. These presses produce one coin at a time. They can run at very high speeds, or at slow speeds and at high pressures for producing collector coins.

Some presses used by the United States Mint have been modified to use more than one set of dies at a time. These

Two Lincoln cent obverse dies are set together, enabling the press to strike more than one coin in each cycle.

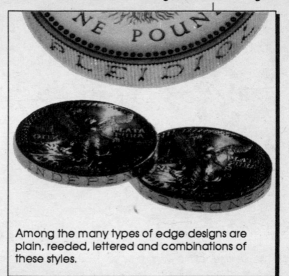

Among the many types of edge designs are plain, reeded, lettered and combinations of these styles.

presses can be set for two or four pairs of dies, and each cycle of the press produces two or four coins. These presses run at moderate speeds. They are used to strike circulating coinage, and the multiple dies are a means of increasing their output.

With each die pair is a **collar**. The collar is a circular piece of steel which forms the wall of a coining chamber, preventing the metal of the coin from spreading out beyond the confines of the dies when it is struck. The collar is sometimes referred to as the third die, because it can impress an image onto a coin's edge. The **reeding** on the half dollars, quarter dollars and dimes of the United States are created with the collar. Similarly, the smooth edges of the cent and 5-cent piece are created by the collar.

More complex edge designs, such as

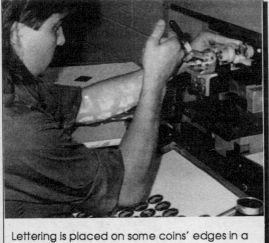

Lettering is placed on some coins' edges in a process separate from striking.

lettering, generally require a separate process, either before or after the coin is struck. Because the metal of the coin expands into the recesses of the collar when the coin is struck, the collar's design must allow the coin to be ejected without interference.

To better understand this, find a coin with a reeded edge, and place it on the table with the obverse up. Remembering that a die is a reverse image of a coin, and that a collar with a design can be considered a die, try to picture what happens when the coin is struck. The metal expands to fill the recesses in the collar. This expansion forms the raised ridges that we call reeding. Because the ridges are perfectly straight up and down, the coin can pop up out of the collar without interference.

Now, if there were letters cut into the

collar, when the metal expanded into the recesses, the collar could not let go of the coin. Either the metal from the coin would be stuck in the collar, or the collar would be stuck in the surrounding coin metal. Therefore, irregular designs must be placed on the coin's edge in a separate step. This is done much like the upsetting mill process above, where the coins are rolled through a machine to impress the design.

Some complex edge designs were attempted in the early days of U.S. coinage. These grew out of the attempt to prevent shaving precious metal from the edges of coins, thereby cheating on a coin's value. Some experiments were made with spring-loaded segmented collars that opened and closed as the dies came together, but the difficulties made them im-

Throughout the world, coins are made in a variety of shapes, often as an aid to identification.

practical for large-scale use.

Many nations issue coins of odd shapes. These can range from triangular to square to many-sided to scalloped (a "frilly" shape). There is at least one practical reason: Irregular shapes help people identify denominations. In countries where illiteracy is high, odd-shaped coins are more common. Collectors enjoy these irregular pieces because they are exotic. Canada even employs non-round coins from time to time. The Loon dollar, for instance, has a rounded, 11-sided shape.

While a coining press is in operation, the press operator inspects finished coins under magnification, looking primarily for defects caused by the dies. Improperly-shaped coins are kept out of circulation by a riddler, which sifts out defective coins.

Like any factory, the Mint makes mistakes, and sometimes these error coins escape into collector's hands. Errors are rare, but can be caused by broken or worn

Error coins are not only interesting, but sometimes reveal information about the manufacturing process.

dies, by loose collars, or by more than one coin being fed between the dies at the time of striking. In some cases, a planchet is fed into the wrong press and struck with the design of another denomination coin. The number of error coins produced is small relative to the number of coins minted in any particular denomination. The number of error coins that make their way out of the Mint and into the hands of collectors is even smaller.

Rarity, though, does not necessarily mean great worth. Some error coins — even unique pieces — can be purchased for a few dollars. The values of error coins depend on the same factors as those for normal coins; supply, demand, and level of preservation.

BEWARE OF an error that appears to be struck on a larger planchet than intended, such as a cent on a 5-cent planchet; larger-than-normal planchets will not fit into the collar to be properly struck.

How paper money is made

Modern U.S. paper money is printed at the Bureau of Engraving and Printing in Washington, D.C. Paper money is printed in sheets of 32 Federal Reserve notes using a three-stage intaglio process. Intaglio is from Italian, meaning "to cut in."

Intaglio printing involves the engraving of steel plates. Each design element is engraved separately by hand. Because the lines carved into the steel will eventually hold the ink to be printed on the paper, the engraver must do all of his work in mirror image. The elements, such as the portrait, framing, vignettes (pictures) and large numbers, are then combined to produce a master plate. The artistry of several engravers may be used on one note design.

The master plate is used to produce

Federal Reserve notes are printed in 32-note sheets, which are cut into 16-note sheets before being overprinted with serial numbers and seals.

working plates, and the working plates are used to print the notes.

Because the plates are engraved, the presses do not merely lay down a design of ink on the paper. Instead, the paper is forced into the ink-filled lines of the plate, leaving a raised line of ink on the paper. By gently sliding the tips of your fingers over the surface of a new Federal Reserve note, you can feel those raised lines.

The green "backs" are printed first, followed by the black note "faces." Sheets are then cut in half and the 16-note half sheets receive the black and green **overprinting** which produces the Treasury and Federal Reserve Bank seals, index numbers and serial numbers, prior to being cut into individual notes.

The intricate manufacturing processes are security measures. The more complex a note is, the harder it is to counterfeit. Future notes of the United States may use such devices as security threads, which are plastic or metallic threads embedded in the paper during the paper manufacturing process. These will be visible when holding a note up to the light. Federal Reserve notes may also use micro-printing, which is extremely fine lettering noticeable only under magnification.

Security is already responsible for much of the way paper money looks and feels. The paper is a special blend of cotton, linen and other fibers. Tiny blue and red fibers are embedded in the paper (look closely, have you ever noticed these before?). The intaglio printing method itself, by being intricate and exacting work, is a security measure.

An engraver works his design — in reverse — directly into a steel plate.

The paper money of other countries can be a colorful and fascinating collecting area. Foreign notes frequently use **watermarks**, which are designs built into the paper by varying the thickness during the paper manufacturing process. These can be seen when the note is held up to the light. Certain notes of Australia are experiments with plastic and **holograms**, which are three-dimensional images.

Knowing how a coin is minted or paper money is printed will help you better understand the origins and significance of money. Looking closely at your money will enable you to appreciate the artistry and craftsmanship that go into its manufacture. You will be able to compare the cultures of the world by comparing their money. And you will learn to distinguish manufacturing characteristics from circulation marks, which is very important when determining the value of your collectible items.

Grading

3

Two factors affect the value of coins: their rarity, and their grade. Between two equally rare coins, the coin with the highest grade will generally be the more valuable. As prices for those often elusive perfect or near-perfect pieces continue to rise, the ability to accurately recognize a coin's grade becomes much more important. Paying for a piece that is overgraded can be expensive and discouraging.

The **grade**, or level of preservation, of a coin describes the amount of wear the coin has sustained since the moment it was manufactured. Coins range in grade from About Good, in which nearly all the designs on the obverse and reverse of the coin are heavily worn or missing, to **Mint State**, or **Uncirculated**, in which the coin is at or near the same level of preservation as when it was minted. Between About Good and Mint State are several additional grades — Good, Fine, Very Fine, Extremely Fine and About Uncirculated — which represent increasing levels of preservation. In addition to these grades, various grades may be further subdivided into grades indicated by numbers.

Grading becomes especially important in the case of Mint State coins. There are as many as 11 grades in Mint State. The scale runs from the lowest Mint State grade, MS-60, up to the MS-70 grade, the grade assigned perfectly flawless pieces. In some cases, grades are split. A grade of MS-60/63, for instance, refers to a Mint State coin with 60 referring to the level of preservation on the obverse side and 63 referring to the level of preservation on the reverse side.

The difference in worth between upper Mint State coins can be thousands of dollars, so it pays to know a coin's condition. For example, in the *1989 Coin World Guide to U.S. Coins, Prices & Value Trends*, a 1932-D Washington quarter dollar, struck at the Denver Mint and graded MS-63, is valued at $685. A 1932-D Washington quarter dollar graded MS-65 is valued at $3,300.

Each coin denomination and year of issue has its own special manufacturing, or striking, characteristics which may affect its grade.

COINS BEGIN TO WEAR as soon as they are struck, when they are ejected from the press into a bin with other new coins.

A number of factors are taken into consideration when looking at Mint State coins: contact marks, luster, strike, toning and color and, most important to the coin collector, eye appeal. Not everyone uses all the factors when they grade coins.

Contact marks, often referred to as "bag marks," are minor abrasions on an otherwise Uncirculated coin. After coins are manufactured at the Mint, the coins are counted, sewn into cloth bags and then shipped to Federal Reserve Banks. The marks are caused by the coins hitting against each other in Mint-sewn bags, or by contact with other surfaces. The size, number and location of contact marks on a coin affect its grade.

Contact marks can occur from normal handling.

Having a coin with a large number of contact marks will probably be unappealing to you. A small mark on a coin with a large diameter might go unnoticed unless placed under a magnifying lens. A large mark on a smaller-diameter coin will be more noticeable.

Another consideration is luster. **Luster** is the quality of a coin's surface, the result of light reflected from microscopic flow lines in the metal from which the coin is produced. When the pictures or designs are placed on the obverse and reverse in the manufacturing process, the metal in the planchet, or blank, flattens and spreads out. **Flow lines** result as the metal follows the outline of the picture being placed on the planchet to produce a coin. Coins with full luster generally have a bright surface, although toning, to be discussed shortly, can affect luster.

Any disturbance to the luster will affect the way light reflects off the surface. A coin whose luster has been disturbed may appear dull. Coins that are circulated do not exhibit luster because the microscopic flow lines have been worn away.

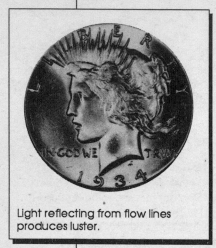

Light reflecting from flow lines produces luster.

Luster on Mint State coins appears somewhat frosty in appearance as opposed to the mirror-like surface of Proof coins. Again, as discussed in the opening chapter, a Proof coin is one that is manufactured on specially-prepared metal planchets, or blanks, on special presses to receive the highest quality strike possible. Proof coins are produced especially for collectors.

A coin's **strike** refers to the sharpness of detail in the coin at the time it leaves the coin press. The strike occurs when the dies — hard metal punches that contain the obverse and reverse designs — press or strike the pictures into opposite sides of the planchets.

How much pressure is exerted at the time the dies strike the designs into the planchet, the condition of the planchet itself, the placement of the planchet to receive the impression of the dies, the amount of wear on the designs on the dies and the complexity of the designs can all affect the strike. A coin with a sharp strike contains clear details in the obverse and reverse designs and legends.

The sharpness of strike on a particular coin can affect the coin's grade, value or both, depending on who is inspecting the coin and what criteria they use.

Toning and color are also important in determining a coin's grade and value. A coin's original color may change over time in reaction to environmental factors. Copper coins, for instance, originally red in color, may turn brown or, depending on environmental influences, even green. Silver coins can change to any number of colors in the rainbow. It is not uncommon to see offered for sale silver half dimes, dimes, 20-cent pieces, quarter dollars, half dollars and dollars that have toned blue, pink, purple or shades of these and other colors.

Because gold is a more stable metal, it is rarely affected by environmental influences. Gold coins salvaged from treasure ships sunk hundreds of years ago in the ocean are still as bright and shiny as the day they were manufactured.

Rainbow toning is now considered desirable by many coin collectors and attractively, naturally-toned coins can be worth more and bring higher prices.

Unscrupulous individuals may artificially tone a coin using a variety of methods in an attempt to deceive the buyer into purchasing such a "beautiful-looking coin."

You may find it difficult at first to tell the difference between a coin that is naturally-toned and one that has been artificially-toned. After you have looked over many coins, you will be able to notice the difference between the two. A coin that has been artificially toned will be worth less, because artificial toning is considered an alteration.

While looking for coins to add to your collection, you may find coins that are worn, yet appear to have a brilliant sur-

OLD COPPER coins may develop a green color, called "verdigris," from the French for "green of the Greeks."

face. In some cases, such coins have been **"dipped,"** treated with chemicals to remove what was once believed to be an unattractive surface for the coin. Dipping strips the outer surface off the coin and restores the brilliance but removes some of the metal in the process.

Despite the importance that accurate grading has for coin collecting, there is no one grading standard on which every collector or dealer can agree. The grading controversy lies between the grade assigned a particular coin by the dealer and the grade an individual might assign to the same coin. Ultimately, the value of a coin is determined by eye appeal. **Eye appeal** pertains to a coin's overall attractiveness, taking into consideration all the grading factors previously discussed. The eye appeal you believe a certain coin has will be as different from another coin collector's eye appeal as his fingerprints. When examining a coin, you must decide how attractive it is to your eye and whether you feel the coin is appealing enough, all things considered, to pay the price being asked to acquire the coin for your collection.

A FINGERPRINT on the surface of a coin detracts from its eye appeal, even though the coin may show no wear.

There are a number of numismatic publications that can assist you in learning about grading. The American Numismatic Association, an association of more than 30,000 collectors of coins and other numismatic material, published the *Official American Numismatic Association Grading Standards for United States Coins,* which contains photographs of the coins to help you.

Brown and Dunn's Guide to the Grading of United States Coins uses drawings to illustrate the various grades. *Photograde* by James F. Ruddy makes use of actual photographs of the coins for each grade discussed.

Numismatic Certification Institute's *The NCI Grading Guide* by James L. Halperin contains photographs of coins and coin maps with colored areas to highlight areas on the coins where wear, contact marks and other disturbances can affect a coin's grade.

EXPERTS AGREE that the best way to learn grading is to examine a large number of coins.

If you're collecting U.S. coins, you should become familiar with at least one of the four grading guides mentioned, but should not ignore the advice of collector friends who have years of experience in grading coins.

Another aspect of grading that you should be aware of is the advent of **grading services** that will grade your coins for a fee.

The **International Numismatic Society Authentication Bureau** (INSAB) in Washington, D.C., began grading coins in 1976 and three years later the **American Numismatic Association Certification Service** (ANACS) began its grading service. ANACS and INSAB will grade your coin and provide a color photo containing the certified grade of the coin.

A number of privately-operated grading services have sprouted up over the years, most notably the **Professional Coin Grading Service** (PCGS) in Newport Beach,

The "slab" is a relatively recent development.

Calif., **Numismatic Guaranty Corporation of America** (NGC) in Parsippany, N.J., and the **Numismatic Certification Service** (NCI) in Dallas, Texas.

Encapsulated or **"slabbed"** coins were introduced to the coin collecting world by PCGS in February 1986 as a solution to the grading controversy. NGC and NCI also offer slabbed coins and ANACS and INSAB began offering the service in 1989. A slabbed coin is one that has been sent to a grading service, examined by one or more numismatists, assigned a grade and then placed in a sealed, plastic holder or "slab" that also contains a slip of paper identifying the type of coin and grade.

The slab also contains numbers used to identify a specific coin and can be used to track a coin if it changes hands. Slabbed coins are usually Mint State or Proof coins.

Slabs are sometimes traded by dealers and investors "sight-unseen"; that is, they are bought and sold without the buyer ever having to see the coin, assured that the grade assigned the coin truly represents its level of preservation. The price paid for a coin graded and then placed into a plastic slab is usually higher than that for the same coin in the "raw" stage, outside a holder.

Unlike the individual who buys high-grade or rare coins strictly as an investment, coin collectors often prefer "raw" coins because in that state the coin's edge, is clearly visible and can be inspected for impairments the collector feels may lower the value of a coin.

Be aware that the grade assigned to a coin by one service may not be the same grade assigned by another service inspecting the same coin. Grading guidelines may differ from grading service to grading service, or different services may interpret the same guidelines more conservatively or more loosely,

In addition to grading coins, services such as ANACS and INSAB will, again for a fee, authenticate coins. Discovering that a coin you just purchased is a complete fake or is a genuine coin altered to resemble a more valuable coin is enough to make anyone want to give up coin collecting and look for another hobby. Unfortunately, it is likely counterfeit and altered coins will continue to be found in the numismatic market in the future.

A **counterfeit** coin is a total fake, produced outside the government Mint which issued the real coin.

An **altered** coin is a genuine coin of lower value, which is then altered — through the removal or addition of a Mint mark, or the alteration of a date, for example — to resemble a rarer and thus

FEW COUNTER-FEITS are good enough to fool the experts; they are usually intended to mislead the inexperienced or unwary.

more expensive coin.

For instance, someone might take a genuine 1922-D Lincoln cent in Good condition and remove the "D" Mint mark identifying the piece as having been manufactured at the Denver Mint. The genuine 1922-D cent with the Mint mark is worth $3.35 in Good condition. The genuine 1922 "Plain" cent, minus the Mint mark, is worth $130.

A related bogus numismatic item, the **replica**, is generally a cast copy of some non-U.S. Mint coin or token or paper copy of a non-federal note produced as a souvenir. Both items turn up with regularity in dealers' junk boxes.

THE HOBBY PROTECTION ACT requires reproductions or imitations of coins and other numismatic items to be permanently marked with the word "COPY."

A beginning collector should not let the possibility of acquiring a counterfeit or an altered coin prevent him from enjoying coin collecting as it was meant to be enjoyed. Professional coin dealers can help you acquire experience in detecting counterfeits. Reputable dealers have developed expertise through years of working with thousands of coins. A dealer who fails to develop a working knowledge of coin authentication will drive himself out of business by his own ignorance. Deal only with reputable, knowledgeable dealers. Pass up opportunities that seem to good to be true. They probably are.

If you have doubts about the authenticity of a particular coin, send it to one of the major authentication services, such as the American Numismatic Association Certification Service (818 North Cascade Ave., Colorado Springs, Colo. 80901; telephone (719) 632-2646); or International Numismatic Society Authentication Bureau (Box 66555, Washington, D.C. 20035; telephone

This dime has been made to appear as a valuable error by impressing the reverse of a cent into clear glue.

(202) 223-4496).

Many dealers are willing to send coins to such services, with instructions that the service make out certificates of authenticity and send them, along with the coins, directly to the collector if the coin is judged genuine. If the service decides the coin is not genuine, it is returned to the dealer and the collector's money is refunded.

Some specialty coin collecting clubs whose members have similar collecting interests — such as those focusing on Civil War tokens, early American Colonial coins, error and variety coins — often offer authentication services free to members only. Check with the organization or firm as to the services provided and specific charges.

Books that may help you in learning

COLLECTORS
OF ERROR
coins or
notes must
be
especially
aware of
authenticity.

about counterfeits and altered coins and paper money are Don Taxay's *Counterfeits, Mis- struck and Unofficial U.S. Coins*, Bert Harshe's *How to Detect Altered & Counterfeit Coins and Paper Money*, and *The Official Guide to Detecting Altered & Counterfeit U.S. Coins & Currency* by Mark Hudgeons.

In addition to these sources of information, serious collectors may at some point wish to consider attending a training seminar on counterfeit detection and grading. Each summer the ANA provides a very popular seminar on this subject.

You should get what you pay for. Being aware of what you are buying and its level of preservation can save you a lot of money and anguish. If you are new to coin collecting, or if you're on a limited budget, you may want to start your collection with coins in lower grades, replacing them with coins in higher grades as you gain expertise.

Finally, as you develop your collection, learn all you can about the minting process. An educated collector is the numismatic counterfeiter's worst enemy. As in any other endeavor, experience is a valuable teacher.

Guide to grading terms

The following guides are not presented as grading standards, but as introductions to the terminology of grading and its usage.

A few words regarding grading usage. When two grades are linked together by a slash — as in Mint State 65/63 — it means that the coin has two grades; the first grade represents the obverse and the second, the reverse. When two grades are linked by a hyphen — as in Mint State 65-63 — it means that the grade for both sides is indeterminate and lies somewhere between the two grades given. Sometimes, a combination of both usages will appear, as in MS-60/60-63, meaning the obverse grades MS-60 and the reverse somewhere between MS-60 and MS-63.

Plus signs (+) are used by many to indicate a coin slightly better than the numerical grade indicated, but not as good as the next numerical grade. A coin graded MS-60+ is better than an MS-60 coin, but not as good as an MS-61 coin.

Many dealers and collectors use adjectives instead of numerals, or combine adjectives and numerals when speaking about Mint State coins. A superb or superb gem coin is generally MS-67, and a gem coin is usually MS-65. Some dealers use choice to describe an MS-63 coin, and others use choice for an MS-65 coin. Mint State 60 coins are generally referred to as Uncirculated or Brilliant Uncirculated; sometimes an MS-60 coin is called typical Uncirculated. Collectors should determine what adjectival "system" the dealer uses when no numerals are present because of the disagreement over what the adjectives represent numerically.

Buyers should remember that different dealers and different collectors or investors use different grading systems. Even though various grading services use an 11-point Mint State system, this does not necessarily mean they use the same criteria for assigning grades. In fact, there is no universally-accepted standard for determining grades for U.S. coins.

Proof: Traditionally, Proof describes a method of manufacture only, and not a grade. However, since numerals are often assigned to Proof coins, there are different qualities of Proof coins; in effect, different grades. A circulated Proof is often called an "impaired Proof." Proof is rarely abbreviated.

Mint State and Uncirculated: The two terms are interchangeable and describe a coin which has no wear. To qualify as Mint State, a coin may not have any level of wear. Even the slightest amount of wear will drop the coin into the About Uncirculated level. (Also, coins described by some dealers as "Borderline Uncirculated" have wear and are actually About Uncirculated.) Mint State is most often used with numerals. The numerical Mint State system so widely used in the current rare coin market is based on a system created by Dr. William H. Sheldon for the U.S. large cents of 1793-1814. It has since spread to U.S. coins in general. Uncirculated is usually abbreviated as Unc.; it often appears as Brilliant Uncirculated, abbreviated as BU. Sometimes used with numerals, generally as Unc. 60, and so on.

About Uncirculated: This is a coin with only the barest traces of wear on the highest points of the design. It is abbreviated AU and often appears with numerals as AU-50, AU-55 and AU-58. The term has gained acceptance despite seeming inconsistency. Some people in the hobby still say that no coin can be About Uncirculated — it is either Uncirculated or it's not. Some use Almost Uncirculated, although all major U.S. grading guides use "About."

Extremely Fine: Light overall wear on highest points, but with all design elements sharp and clear. It is abbreviated by most hobbyists as EF, although a few use XF. It appears as EF-40 and EF-45.

Very Fine: The coin has light to moderate even wear on surface and high points of design. Abbreviated VF, it appears with numerals as VF-20 and VF-30. The abbreviations VF-25 and VF-35 are infrequently used.

Fine: The wear is considerable although the entire design is still strong and visible. It is abbreviated as F-12.

Very Good: The design and surface are well worn, main features are clear but flat. Abbreviated as VG, it is used with numeral as VG-8 and VG-10.

Good: Design and surface are heavily worn, with some details weak and many details flat. It is abbreviated only when used with numeral, G-4; G-6 is infrequently used. Ironically, a coin in Good condition is not a "good" coin to collect; a Good coin is generally the lowest collectible grade.

About Good: The design is heavily worn with surface fading into rim, many details weak or missing. Abbreviated as AG, it is used with a numeral as AG-3. Few coins are collectible in About Good condition. Dealers also use the terms Fair and Fair 3 to describe a coin in this state of preservation.

Paper money terms:

New and **Uncirculated** — Terms are interchangeable, and often preceded by "Crisp." A new note cannot show any folds, creases or tears, but may show bank teller handling, including pinholes. Notes that have the image well-centered on each side and even margins bring a premium over more typical notes. Crisp Uncirculated is abbreviated CU.

Extremely Fine — Must retain crispness, but may have a light center fold or light corner fold, no major tears or stains. Abbreviated EF or sometimes XF.

Very Fine — Some crispness must remain, two to four folds or corner creases, but no tears. Has seen moderate circulation, but still attractive to the eye and to the touch. Several small stains or one larger stain are permitted, but should not detract from the general appearance of the note. Abbreviated VF.

Fine — Horizontal and vertical folds and creases are well-defined. Most of the crispness is gone, some limpness may be noticeable. Seen considerable circulation and may have one or two minor tears. It may have some larger, more noticeable stains detracting from the note's general appearance. Generally not abbreviated.

Very Good — Well-worn, with considerable folding and limpness. Note may be dirty, but not filthy. The print may have worn away along the heavy creases.

Good — Note is ragged and dirty, and may have holes, large tears, missing corners and considerable wear and damage.

Other common grading terms:

Fleur de Coin — Often used for foreign coins, it is basically the same as Uncirculated.

Mediocre — For ancient coins, the coin is identifiable, with some design still recognizable.

Poor — For ancient coins, heavily damaged or corroded, perhaps not even identifiable.

Storing and handling

4

Good judgment alone dictates that coins should not be abused, mishandled or stored loosely with other coins in a way that can cause dents, nicks or scratches.

How you pick up your coins is important. Handle your coins as little as possible, but when you must handle them, never pick them up with your fingers touching the obverse or reverse sides of the coin. Dirt and other contaminants on your hands, not to mention the natural oils of your skin, can react with the surface metal of the coin and cause irreversible damage. The only proper way to handle a coin is by placing the coin between the thumb and forefinger, holding the edge of the coin and rotating it between those fingers to inspect its various details. You may even want to purchase an inexpensive pair of cotton gloves to avoid transferring any contaminants from your hands to your coins. Grading services always use such precautions when handling customers' coins.

Don't breathe directly on your coins.

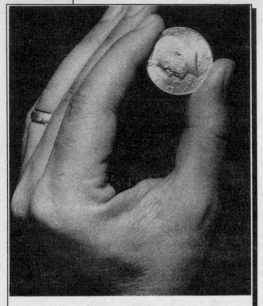

Learn to handle your coins without risking damage to them.

This may sound humorous to the beginning collector, but advanced hobbyists know that warm, moist breath can affect the surfaces of coins, especially the delicate surfaces of Proof coins.

When examining your coins, use a velvet or velvet-like padded mat, similar to those you might see in a jeweler's display case. Place the mat flat on a table to catch any coin that might happen to fall out of its holder while you are handling it. Make sure the pad is thick enough to completely cushion a coin's unanticipated fall. Gold coins in particular are very soft, and dropping them on a hard surface can result in permanent damage that detracts from their beauty and value. This extra care can help you avoid adding dents, scratches and other unwanted blemishes to your coins.

Many collectors and investors are tempted to clean their coins. Each year, countless numbers of coins are ruined forever by misguided attempts at cleaning. Coins that have been handled improperly or have suffered corrosion or other reactions to the environment can be cleaned, but in many cases this is a job for experts. Collectors never want coins in their collection that show even the slightest hint of having been cleaned.

Ideally, coins should look as if they have been preserved in their natural state. When coins are originally new and bright, you should of course attempt to keep them at that level of preservation. But keep in mind that circulated coins which have their original Mint sheen worn away can never have this luster restored. No amount of polishing or cleaning will make a new coin out of one that has been in circulation, and stripping the outside film (called the **patina**, in the case of copper or silver coins) that naturally develops on a coin after a number of years will only leave the coin's surface exposed to further and possibly more serious damage.

Keep in mind, too, that natural toning is considered an attractive feature to many collectors — so much so that some unscrupulous individuals attempt to create toning artificially. In any case, most collectors prefer coins showing the darkening of age or natural toning over coins that have been stripped of these features by improper cleaning. Coins that have been naturally toned should be left alone.

THE ACT OF using a wire brush to "shine up" a coin is called "whizzing."

Coins that have been subjected to chemical cleaners are said to have been **"dipped."** Dipping strips off surface metal from a coin and leaves the coin with a shiny but unnatural finish. Collectors avoid dipped coins, because there is no way of knowing how many times a coin has been dipped before it has been offered for sale.

GOLD IS VERY RESISTANT to tarnish, but smokers beware! Tobacco can stain gold.

Does all this mean you yourself should never under any circumstances attempt to clean coins that have accumulated dirt, been smudged, or which are tarnished? Not at all — but you should exercise caution, especially in the case of rare or valuable coins. Loose dirt can generally be removed by carefully washing coins with a good-quality soap, after which they should be patted dry with a soft tissue. Coins should never be brushed or rubbed with any abrasive or rough object, which can cause the removal of surface metal and lessen the value of the coin.

There are a number of commercial coin cleansers available. If you wish to use them, experiment first on coins of no special value, and then use them on valuable coins only after you have gained experience and if, in the opinion of an expert, such cleaning would be to your advantage.

Perhaps the best advice that can be given with regard to cleaning coins is to avoid the necessity for it. In addition to handling coins properly, that means storing them to prevent, or at least greatly slow down, the natural processes of oxidation and surface decay that result from exposure to the environment.

A wide spectrum of storage devices is available. At one end of the spectrum are devices designed for easy viewing and access or short-term storage; at the other end of the spectrum are long-term storage devices designed to preserve coins in a natural condition indefinitely.

Chances are, the coin you purchased from the dealer at your local coin shop or at a coin show came in a holder that is not suitable for long-term storage. Many of the less-expensive coins in a dealer's inventory are kept in thin plastic pockets slipped inside small paper envelopes. Another popular device for storing individual coins in dealers' inventories consists of small folded cardboard holders with clear plastic windows in the middle so you can see the obverse and reverse of the coin. These holders can be stapled shut on all four sides, sealing the coin between the sides of the holder. The windows are of varying sizes to accommodate the various denominations of coins to be stored. Information about the coins can be written on the outside.

Some of these paper holders are undesirable because they contain sulfur in sufficient quantity to react with the surface metal on your coin, reducing its level of preservation and value.

A similar problem exists in the case of some plastic coin **"flips."** Flips come in different sizes to hold different coin denominations. Each flip has two sides, which fold over, and each side has a pocket. One pocket holds the coin, the other a paper insert that can be written on to indicate pertinent information about the coin. Flips are convenient short-term storage devices, frequently used by dealers at coin conventions or shows because they are soft and pliable and allow all three sides of the coin

WHILE COINS are quite durable for circulation, their surfaces are delicate.

There are many types of holders available to the collector.

to be easily viewed. Some flips, though, contain **polyvinylchloride**, otherwise known as **"PVC."** It wasn't until several years after the introduction of flips containing PVC that dealers and collectors began noticing a greenish or blue slime or stain on many of their coins.

The discoloration was found to be permanent in many instances. In addition, removing the coins from these holders after years of storage sometimes resulted in part of the holder sticking to the surface of the coin, causing further damage. It was found that chemicals in the PVC were bleeding out of the film onto the coins. Many collectors like to remove the coin from the PVC flip and place it into another flip, one containing no PVC or other chemical that will react with the metal in the coin and cause damage.

Some coin folders that house coins like a fold-out book, as well as coin tubes to store rolls of coins, also contain PVC. Other holders for long-term storage are made of acrylic or plastic, especially those seen on the bourse floor housing earlier dated Uncirculated and Proof sets. The 2-

by-2-inch polystyrene holders are of convenient storage size, and are suitable for display purposes in coin exhibits. Their special construction offers nearly complete protection for an indefinite period of time.

Slabs, those specially-sealed plastic holders housing mostly Uncirculated and Proof coins graded by grading services, are also considered long-term storage holders. Still another popular holder is made of triacetate with two circular halves that snap together with the coin snug in between. There are other similar snap-together plastic holders in varying shapes and sizes.

Clear plastic sandwich-type holders are also popular. Available in a variety of shapes and sizes to accommodate individual coins or sets, these devices are held together with plastic screws around the perimeter, securing the two halves of the holder and the center insert.

The value and level of preservation of the coin or coins you have purchased will have a lot to do with making the decision about the means of storage you want to follow. Circulated coins are not at risk to the same degree as Uncirculated or Proof coins. Keep in mind, though that whatever kind of coins you collect, improper storage can cost you your collection.

Remember, too, that no matter how well you preserve your coins, they will be subject to oxidation and tarnish when exposed to normal environmental conditions. Collectors living in areas with high levels of air pollution or excessive humidity must take extra precautions in caring for their collections. In coastal areas, salt air can be

HEAT AND SUNLIGHT can speed up chemical reactions and damage your collectibles.

BECAUSE CONTAMINANTS may be embedded in the coin's metal, even airtight seals are no guarantee against corrosion.

particularly corrosive. The only sure way to preserve a coin in its natural condition is to keep it embedded in some kind of plastic, or sealed in a completely air-tight container. The drawback to this kind of storage is in not being able to get to the coin when you want to examine or display it.

You want to use a holder that will best preserve each coin in your collection while allowing easy access, and you don't want to have to keep switching your coins from holder to holder. Excessive handling of your coins can cause just as much damage as putting the coins in the wrong kind of holder. Any of the 2-by-2-inch or similar size coin holders for individual coins can be stored in cardboard or plastic slide trays or storage boxes. Boxes and trays come in single- and double-row sizes and allow storage of a large number of individual coins. The boxes and trays also allow you to transport a large number of coins conveniently. Care should be taken to select a type of box or tray that is as airtight as possible.

In addition to the storage methods already discussed, pressed board coin folders and albums are popular with beginning collectors for housing circulated coins in lower grades. These holders, which are manufactured by specific coin type, issue and denomination, allow you to press your coins in place in each of the openings of each page. The openings to accommodate each coin are arranged by date and Mint mark, and on some folders have the mintage of that particular issue printed below the opening. While this kind of holder is very popular among beginners, it only allows you to see one side of the coin, either obverse or reverse, depending on which side is facing out.

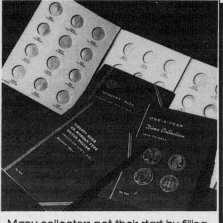

Be careful about storing coins in folders or albums that have see-through slides or windows. Moving these slides or windows back and forth can, over

Many collectors got their start by filling a coin album.

time, cause wear marks on the high points on the surfaces of your coins. You can store rolls of coins of plastic coin tubes sealed with tape to prevent the tops from accidentally falling off and spilling out the contents.

Collectors of paper money should exercise the same common-sense cautions that apply to coins. They must also take care not to fold, crease or tear the paper items, as all of these will reduce its value.

Also, collectible paper items that may be torn should never be taped, and marks should not be erased.

A few highly trained specialists have the know-how to neutralize acidic papers and clean valuable items. Attempting to do so without the proper training can permanently ruin your valuable collectible.

Where you store your collection is as important as what you store your collection in. Avoid subjecting coins, paper money and other numismatic items to extremes of moisture, heat, or direct sunlight, as these can speed up the natural processes of decay or impairment. The goal of storing coins is to keep your coins in as secure an airtight environment as possible to protect them from contaminants that may be floating in the air. It is important you store your coins in a cool, dry place. Dampness and humidity can cause surface damage and corrosion to your coins. The kind and extent of damage depends on the severity of dampness and humidity and the coin's metal content. Storing silica gel along with the coins to remove moisture, especially if you live in a humid environment, may prove helpful. Many numismatic supply companies offer specially formulated moisture inhibitors that cost only a few dollars and are well worth the investment.

PAPER MONEY should not be stored in basements, or in any place where molds can develop.

It is also recommended that you maintain a written record of your collection. The record should describe each item, where it was purchased, its condition at time of purchase, and the price. It is fine to keep this record with your collection, but you should also keep a copy in a safe place separate from the collection. That way, if your collection is stolen, you will have a complete record to supply to authorities, and for insurance purposes.

Finally, no matter how or where you store your coins, be sure to inspect them occasionally to see that no harmful tarnish has developed. It is an unusual collector who does not enjoy looking at his coin collection from time to time.

Coins are not as indestructible as most people think. They are delicate works of art that should be handled accordingly. The slightest mistake could prove very expensive. Knowing and practicing the basics of proper handling and storage is a big step toward assuring that your coins age the way they were meant to age.

Security should concern even the newest collector. Storing your collection at home is ideal if you want to have access to your coins at a moment's notice, but it may not always be safe. Since coins and paper money are currency, and usable as a medium of exchange, they are attractive to thieves for their face value alone.

Some collectors keep their coins in a safe at home, or hide them so they have convenient access to their collection. As for hiding your coins, remember that you are an amateur while the person from whom you wish to hide them may be a professional. It is highly doubtful that you will fool him for long.

Security measures such as deadbolt locks on doors, locks on windows, alarms and other means of protection for your collection should be considered as you would consider your home's protection without a coin collection. If you do leave your collection at home, remember that no technique is positive prevention against a professional thief. The history of thefts from major "secure" museum and private collections should be ample proof of this.

It is wise to be discreet about your

IT IS FUN TO DISPLAY items from your collection, but take care not to attract the attention of the wrong person.

home collection. Most of us enjoy sharing our hobby with others, making total discretion difficult. Still, there are a few common-sense steps you can take to address this problem. When buying or selling coins through the mail, for instance, it's smart not to advertise on the outside of an envelope that you are a coin collector. Some collectors request that dealers from whom they purchase coins not print the name of their business on their envelopes. Many collectors rent a post office box and have all correspondence dealing with coins sent to that address rather than to their home address.

IF YOU MAKE frequent visits to your safe-deposit box, vary your routine so as not to attract the attention of professional thieves.

If your coin collection contains coins of considerable worth, you may want to consider storing them in a safe-deposit box at your local bank. Selecting the right kind of safe-deposit room is important. A safe-deposit box room that is air-conditioned and climate-controlled is considered best. You may want to avoid one which has an ozone purification system. Such a system emits a germ-killing agent that will corrode certain kinds of coins very quickly. If you do decide to put your coins in a bank's safe-deposit box, read the rental agreement carefully. The agreement spells out the terms and the liability on the bank's part should something happen to your collection.

Based on the value of your collection as it grows, you may decide that you should have a home safe in which to temporarily store those items on which you are working until you can return them to the bank.

Whether you keep your coins at home

or at a bank, make it a point to check with your insurance agent about what type of coverage is needed to protect your collection. Keep a descriptive list of your coins, and photographs of the more valuable pieces, in a safe place away from where the coins are stored as an added protection in the event of theft or natural disaster.

As a collector, an investor, or both, it will do little good to use sound judgment in putting together a collection or portfolio only to see your efforts wiped out as the result of careless handling, improper storage, or theft.

RARE COINS should be preserved for the next generation of collectors.

Building a library

Every coin collector and investor should have a numismatic library, whether it includes a few, carefully-chosen books or an extensive collection of volumes covering a variety of numismatic topics. A well-chosen numismatic library is necessary for the full enjoyment of coin collecting. You will find yourself turning often from your collection to your library as your thirst for numismatic knowledge grows.

Coins reflect man's history. Numismatic books record that history with a numismatic perspective. Your collecting interests help direct you to the right reference works. At the same time, reference works can help you decide what direction your collection will take.

A good place to start looking for reference works is in the classified advertisements printed weekly in *Coin World*. You will also find dealers offering the latest in numismatic books. Many of the dealers who advertise in the classifieds specialize in such books. Purchasing books through these ads can introduce you to book specialists. Book specialists not only offer books at competitive prices to fit the budgets of most collectors, but also offer, usually through mail-bid sale or auction, out-of-date reference books that often command high prices.

Other sources for numismatic books include your local coin dealer, newsstands and bookstores. Should the book you want not be in stock at any of these establishments, they may be able to order it for you from a book wholesaler, or directly from the publisher.

FINDING THE RIGHT reference book can be as challenging as finding the right coin.

Coin shows are another source of reference materials. Coin dealers often bring books for sale with them to coin shows, and book specialists normally attend the larger coin conventions.

A valuable reference source that is often overlooked is the auction catalog. The larger numismatic auction houses devote a large amount of energy and resources to producing catalogs for auctions.

These auction catalogs are generally well-illustrated, often with full color pages as well as black and white. Professional numismatists describe the principal lots in great detail.

Subscribing to the catalogs of one or two auction houses is reasonable. You will find firms that tend to offer the type of material you are interested in. You can then use the catalogs as valuable references. By tracking the prices realized, which are generally available after the results of the auction are compiled, you have an accurate source for determining the value of certain types of material.

Visit your local library to see what kinds of numismatic books it has on its shelves. Major public libraries and libraries on college campuses usually have selections of numismatic books. You will find most librarians happy to accept suggestions and recommendations for books they may want to buy for their libraries.

Being able to check out a numismatic book from your local library for a few weeks often can help you decide whether you want to purchase the book for your home library. Remember, too, that many local coin clubs have a library with books available for members to borrow.

One advantage of membership in the American Numismatic Association is that the ANA maintains the world's largest free, circulating numismatic library.

The ANA library has more than 35,000 circulating volumes. Most of these are available for only a few dollars each to

Collectors can find books about every numismatic subject.

SPECIALTY CLUBS often maintain their own reference libraries for use by members.

cover postage and insurance both ways. Rarer reference works which are not available for loan can, in some instances, be used in the ANA library itself if you are fortunate enough to arrange a visit to ANA headquarters in Colorado Springs, Colo. Volumes available in the ANA Library cover all aspects of United States and world numismatics: coins, paper money, tokens, medals, orders and decorations, and stocks and bonds.

In addition to books, you will find one of the finest selections of auction catalogs in the world plus a wide range of numismatic periodicals, including nearly 30 years of *Coin World* on microfilm. The ANA Library catalog, covering several hundred pages, provides a complete listing of numismatic literature.

The books discussed on the following pages are used often by *Coin World* staff writers when researching information for articles. Some of the books are out of print, though available through numismatic book dealers. Other older volumes have been reprinted in modern editions.

For beginning collectors especially, these inexpensive reprints are recommended over the expensive original editions. Some of the original editions are hundreds of years old and collectors' items themselves.

U.S., general

The 336-page, pocket-sized *Coin World Guide to U.S. Coins, Prices & Value Trends*, introduced in 1989, presents for the first time in book form, price performance graphs tracking more than 16,576 United States coin values. Written by *Coin World* News Editor William T. Gibbs, with coin Trends values compiled by *Coin World* Trends Editor Keith M. Zaner, the book provides a straight-forward approach to collecting and investing in U.S. coins, containing essential information about rarity, grading, pricing, buying and selling coins, and the performance of individual coin issues in the numismatic market. Also included in the book is capsule information about coins series and types, along with actual-size photographs for you to quickly and easily identify U.S. coins. The book, to be published annually with updated information, comprises 14 chapters, including a glossary of numismatic terms; a unified history of U.S. coins, divided into sections covering denominations, specifications and designs; a brief history of the U.S. Mints, with information about locating Mint marks; grading; the cyclical nature of the coin market; mintage figures; error coins; "mysterious rarities," defined as those pieces with mysterious origins such as the 1804 dollar and 1913 Liberty Head 5 cents; and "necessity money," covering the pre-federal coinages,

Hard Times and Civil War token issues, and pioneer gold coins.

Walter Breen's Complete Encyclopedia of U.S. and Colonial Coins, published in 1988 by Doubleday, fills 754 pages and is illustrated with more than 4,000 photographs. Considered the definitive U.S. numismatic reference book, Breen's book explores coin issues from Colonial pieces to modern U.S. commemoratives. The book describes in detail every major and minor U.S. coin, including the first brass Bermuda shillings issued in 1616 to such recent issues as the State of Liberty commemorative coins in 1986. According to Doubleday, the more than 7,800 entries in Breen's book represent more than four times as much information as can be found in any other book of its kind.

Other books to consider:

Annual Report of the Director of the Mint. United States Mint, Department of the Treasury, issued annually. A valuable source for numismatists, with mintage figures, photographs of new coins and medals, reports about new coinage programs, reports about technology changes at the Mint, charts about gold and silver deposits to the Mint and more. May be ordered from the United States Mint, Treasury Department, Washington, D.C. 20220.

Coin World Almanac. Staff of Coin World. Amos Press Inc., Sidney, Ohio 45365. 1987. One-volume general reference, includes chronologies of United States and world numismatics; history of precious metals; legal issues relating to coinage; other sections relating to collecting coins and paper money. Four earlier editions, dated 1976, 1977, 1978 and 1984.

The Coin Collector's Survival Manual. **Travers, Scott A.** Second edition, 1988, Prentice Hall Press, New York. First edition, 1984, Arco Publishing, Inc., New York. Includes ways of refining your method of looking at coins; grading; grading services; telling Proof from prooflike; how to get the most out of price guides; guarantees and mail-order coin buying; the role of the coin convention; how to sell your coins; cleaning coins; how to choose the right coin holder; and safekeeping of your coins.

The Catalogue & Encyclopedia of U.S. Coins. **Taxay, Don.** Scott Publishing, New York, 1976. Includes patterns, rarity ratings for many pieces, pedigrees of rarer coins and all regular issues, commemoratives, Colonials, state issues and pioneer gold.

A Guide Book of United States Coins. **Yeoman, R.S.** Western Publishing Company, Racine, Wis., annually since 1947. Basic catalog listing of U.S. Colonial, state, Mint and commemorative coins, plus pioneer gold; the "Red Book."

A Handbook of United States Coins. **Yeoman, R.S.** Western Publishing Co., Racine, Wis., annually. Formerly hard-cover, now soft-cover, this guide is for the beginning collector of U.S. coins; the "Blue Book."

The History of United States Coinage as Illustrated by the Garrett Collection. **Bowers, Q. David.** Bowers and Ruddy Galleries, Inc., Los Angeles, Calif., 1979. Covers the history of U.S. coins and collecting, with numerous letters and other documents quoted extensively.

The Macmillan Encyclopedic Dictionary of Numismatics. **Doty, Richard G.** Macmillan Publishing Co., New York, 1982. Illustrated dictionary, plus bibliography.

Numismatic Art in America. **Vermeule, Cornelius.** Belknap Press of Harvard University Press, Cambridge, Mass., 1971. Examines the aesthetics of U.S. coinage, and traces development of engraving skills of U.S. engravers.

U.S. Mint and Coinage. **Taxay, Don.** Durst Numismatic Publications, New York, 1983 (reprint of 1966 book). Early history of U.S. Mint and minting processes in detail, plus history from mid-19th century to modern coinage.

Colonial, pioneer, patterns

California Pioneer Fractional Gold. **Breen, Walter, and Gillio, Ronald J.** Pacific Coast Auction Galleries Inc., Santa Barbara, Calif., 1983. Catalog listing of varieties of California fractional gold, including black-and-white photos of most coins.

The Early Coins of America. **Crosby, Sylvester S.** Quarterman Publications Inc., New York, 1983 (facsimile reprint of 1875 book). Covers all Colonial, Confederation and state issues, with extracts from authorizing legislation, plus plates.

Encyclopedia of United States and Colonial Proof Coins 1722-1977. **Breen, Walter.** FCI Press, Inc., Albertson, N.Y., 1977. Historical information and pedigrees about U.S. Proofs, with sections covering branch Mint Proofs and fantasy and restrike pieces.

Private Gold Coins and Patterns of the United States. **Kagin, Donald H.** Arco Publishing Inc., New York, 1981. History and catalog of pioneer gold, excluding fractional parts of a dollar.

United States Pattern, Experimental and Trial Pieces. **Judd, J. Hewitt, and Kosoff, A.** Western Publishing Co. Inc., Racine, Wis., 1982. Covers all non-issued U.S. coin designs in catalog form, with illustrations, pedigrees, rarity ratings and prices.

U.S. copper

American Half Cents. **Cohen, Roger S.**
Wigglesworth & Ghatt Co., Arlington, Va., 1982. Catalog listing of all known half cent varieties, with photos accompanying listings.

America's Copper Coinage 1783-1857.
American Numismatic Society, New York, 1985. Features articles about state and federal copper coinage through the demise of the large cent. Reprints of papers presented at the ANS's 1984 Coinage of the Americas Conference.

Encyclopedia of United States Half Cents 1793-1857. **Breen, Walter.**
American Institute of Numismatic Research, South Gate, Calif., 1984. Historical information and pedigrees, plus catalog listing of all known half cent varieties, with photos accompanying the listings.

The Fugio Cents. Kessler, Alan. Colony Coin Co., Newtonville, Mass. 1976. A catalog listing of varieties of the United States' first coinage, with historical information.

Penny Whimsy. Sheldon, William H.
Quarterman Publications Inc., Lawrence, Mass., 1983 (Reprint of 1958 edition, 1976 copyright). Catalog listing of known varieties of large cents from 1793 to 1814, with plates in back.

The Two-Cent Piece and Varieties. **Kliman, Myron M.** Sanford J. Durst Numismatic Publications, New York, 1983. Catalog listing of known varieties, with no photos.

United States Copper Cents 1816-1857. **Newcomb, Howard R.** Quarterman Publications Inc, Lawrence, Mass., 1981 (facsimile reprint of 1944 book). Catalog listing of known varieties of later large cents, with plates in back.

United States Copper Coins — An Action Guide for the Collector and Investor. Bowers and Merena Inc., Wolfeboro, N.H., 1984. Covers half cents, large cents, small cents and 2-cent pieces with historical information and investment advice.

U.S. silver

The Comprehensive Catalogue and Encyclopedia of U.S. Morgan and Peace Silver Dollars. **Van Allen, Leroy C., and Mallis, A. George.** Arco Publishing Co., New York, 1976. Historical information and catalog listing of all known varieties.

The Fantastic 1804 Dollar. **Bressett, Kenneth E., and Newman, Eric P.** Whitman Publishing Co., Racine, Wis., 1962. A numismatic mystery is solved in this in-depth study of the 1804 dollar, one of the United States' greatest rarities.

The United States Early Silver Dollars from 1794 to 1803. **Bolender, M.H.** Krause Publications, Iola, Wis., 1980. (Revised reprint of 1950 book.) Catalog listing of dollar varieties, with plates in back.

The United States Trade Dollar. **Willem, John M.** Sanford J. Durst Numismatic Publications, New York, 1983. Historical treatment of the Trade dollar, with mintage by month, varieties and rarity levels.

Early Half Dollar Varieties. **Overton, Al C.** Colorado Springs, Colo., 1970. Catalog listing of all known varieties, with photos accompanying listings.

The Walking Liberty Half Dollar. **Swiatek, Anthony.** Sanford J. Durst Numismatic Publications, New York, 1983. Catalog listing, with emphasis on distinguishing between strong strikes and weak strikes.

The Early Quarter Dollars of the United States. **Browning, A.W.** Sanford J. Durst Numismatic Publications, New York, 1977 (reprint of 1925 book). Catalog listing of known varieties, with plates at back.

Standing Liberty Quarters. **Cline, J.H.** Cline's Rare Coins, Palm Harbor, Fla., 1986. Historical information, including correspondence between designer and Treasury officials, plus catalog listing and investment advice.

Encyclopedia of United States Liberty Seated Dimes. **Ahwash, Kamal M.** Kamal Press, 1977. Catalog listing of known varieties, with over-sized photos accompanying listings.

Early United States Dimes: 1796-1837. **Davis, David J.; Logan, Russell, J.; Lovejoy, Allen F.; McCloskey, John W.; Subjack, William L.** John Reich Collectors Society, 1984. Catalog of known varieties for Draped Bust and Capped Bust dimes, with over-sized photos accompanying listings.

The United States Half Dimes. **Valentine, Daniel W.** Quarterman Publications Inc., Lawrence, Mass., 1975 (reprint of 1931 book). Valentine catalog listing, plus updated information on other individuals.

U.S. gold

United States Gold Coins: An Illustrated History. **Bowers, Q. David.** Bowers and Ruddy Galleries, Los Angeles, 1982. The history of U.S. gold coins.

U.S. Gold Dollars through U.S. Double Eagles. **Akers, David W.** Paramount Publications, Englewood, Ohio, 1975-1982. A series of six books covering gold dollars, quarter eagles, $3 and $4 gold pieces, half eagles, eagles and double eagles; basically it records auction appearances by denomination, date and Mint mark.

United States Gold Patterns. **Akers, David W.** Paramount International Coin Corp., Englewood, Ohio, 1975. Subtitled "A photographic study of the gold patterns struck at the United States Mint from 1836 to 1907."

Tokens, medals

The Atwood-Coffee Catalogue of United States and Canadian Transportation Tokens. **Coffee Jr., John M., and Ford, Harold V.** The American Vecturist Association, Boston, 1983. The book catalogs mass transportation tokens and similar items, based on earlier Atwood systems and catalog. Other volumes catalog minor die varieties and record the history of the transportation token.

Early American Tokens, Hard Times Tokens, U.S. Merchant Tokens 1845-1860, United States Trade Tokens 1866-1889, Tokens of the Gay Nineties 1890-1900. **Rulau, Russell.** Krause Publications, Iola, Wis., 1981-1983. Five volumes in a planned series listing of all U.S. merchant tokens (except Civil War pieces) and related pieces in a soft-cover catalog format.

Medals of the United States Mint — The First Century 1792-1892. **Julian, Robert W.** Token and Medal Society Inc., 1977. Massive historical work covering all medallic works produced by the Mint during its first 100 years.

Patriotic Civil War Tokens. **Fuld, George, and Fuld, Melvin.** Civil War Token Society, 1982 (released 1984). Catalog lists all Civil War patriotic tokens, with historical information and chapters on related topics.

So-Called Dollars. **Hibler, Harold E., and Kappen, Charles V.** The Coin and Currency Institute, New York, 1963. Covers commemorative and exposition medals of near-dollar size in catalog format, listing metal varieties and historical information.

U.S. Civil War Store Cards. **Fuld, George, and Fuld, Melvin.** Quarterman Publications, Lawrence, Mass., 1975. Catalogs all Civil War store cards by city and state, with historical information.

Video Arcade, Pinball, Slot Machine and Other Amusement Tokens of North America. **Alpert, Stephen A., and Smith, Kenneth E.** Amusement Token Collectors Association, Redondo Beach, Calif., 1984. Catalogs all known amusement tokens by state, province and miscellaneous categories.

Counterfeit detection

Counterfeit Detection. **Staff of the American Numismatic Association Certification Service.** American Numismatic Association, Colorado Springs, Colo., two volumes, 1983 and 1987. Reprints ANACS's columns appearing in *The Numismatist*, discussing and illustrating counterfeits and genuine specimens of dozens of U.S. coins, plus information about collectible varieties and ANACS procedures.

Counterfeits of U.S. States Coins. **Spanbauer, Larry.** Service Litho-Print Inc., Oshkosh, Wis., 1975. Illustrates many Colonial, private Mint and modern counterfeits and replicas.

Detecting Counterfeit Coins, Book 1. **Devine, "Lonesome" John.** Heigh Ho Printing Co., Newbury Park, Calif., Illustrates and describes many counterfeit U.S. minor and silver coins.

Detecting Counterfeit Gold Coins, Book 2. **Devine, "Lonesome" John.** Heigh Ho Printing Co., Newbury Park, Calif., 1977. Illustrates and describes many counterfeit gold coins.

Grading

The Accugrade System. **Hager, Alan.** Silver Dollars Unlimited Inc., Bedford, N.Y., 1984, Accugrade Inc., Greenwich, Conn., 1986. A three-volume guide to grading Uncirculated, Proof and prooflike Morgan, Peace and Eisenhower dollars.

Grading Coins: A Collection of Readings. **Edited by Bagg, Richard, and Jelinski, James J.** Essex Publications, Portsmouth, N.H., 1977. Collection of articles about grading from *The Numismatist, Whitman Numismatic Journal* and *Numismatic Scrapbook Magazine* from 1892 to 1976. Takes a historical approach.

A Guide to the Grading of United States Coins. Brown, Martin T., and Dunn, John W. General Distributors Inc., Denison, Texas, 1980. Uses line illustrations for U.S. coins in all denominations from half cent to double eagle in all grades.

NCI Grading Guide. Halperin, James L. Ivy Press, Dallas, Texas, 1986. Written by a principal grader of the Numismatic Certification Institute. Provides a step-by-step approach to the grading of Uncirculated and Proof coins. Does not cover circulated grades.

New Photograde. Ruddy, James F. Bowers and Ruddy Galleries Inc., Los Angeles, 1972. Photographic guide to the grading of U.S. coins in all denominations from half cent to double eagle.

Official American Numismatic Association Grading Standards for United States Coins. Bressett, Kenneth, and Kosoff, A. Whitman Numismatic Products, Western Publishing, Racine, Wis., 1987. Official ANA guide to grading U.S. coins; third edition (1987) uses black-and-white photographs; first two editions use line illustrations. Includes non-illustrated guide to grading U.S. commemorative coins.

Errors, varieties

The Classification and Value of Errors on the Lincoln Cent. **Cohen, Jean.** Bonita Springs, Fla., 1969. Out of print. Illustrates through line drawings minor errors on Lincoln cents and lists their (outdated) values.

The Design Cud. **Marvin, Paul, and Margolis, Arnold.** Heigh Ho Printing Co., Newbury Park, Calif., 1979. In-depth explanation and photographs of how major die breaks, cuds, occur.

The Encyclopedia of Doubled Dies, Vols. 1 and 2. **Wexler, John A.** Robert C. Wilharm News Printing Co., Inc., Fort Worth, Texas, 1978 and 1981. Illustrates and describes doubled dies on U.S. coins, and how they occur.

How Error Coins are Made at the U.S. Mints. **Margolis, Arnold.** Heigh Ho Printing Co., Newbury Park, Calif., 1981. Describes and illustrates how coins are minted and how error coins occur.

Modern Mint Mistakes. **Steiner, Phillip, and Zimpfer, Michael.** Whispering Pines Printing, Ind., 1975-1976. Provides general information and a price guide to error coins.

Official Price Guide to Mint Errors and Varieties. **Herbert, Alan.** House of Collectibles Inc., Orlando, Fla., 1981. Offers a general, overall look at error coins.

The RPM Book. **Wexler, John A., and Miller, Tom.** Lonesome John Publishing Co., Newbury Park, Calif., 1983. Describes and illustrates repunched and over Mint marks, with price information.

Paper money

Bureau of Engraving and Printing — The First Hundred Years 1862-1962. Sanford J. Durst Numismatic Publications, New York, 1978 (reprint of 1962 book published by the Treasury Department). Government history tracing history of BEP and government-issued paper money, postage stamps and revenue items.

The Comprehensive Catalog of U.S. Paper Money. **Hessler, Gene.** BNR Press, Port Clinton, Ohio, 1983. Catalog listings of government issues, with historical information.

The Encyclopedia of United States Fractional and Postal Currency. **Friedberg, Milton.** Numismatic and Antiquarian Service Corporation of America, Long Island, N.Y., 1978. Historical information and catalog of federal fractional notes of Civil War and Reconstruction.

Military Payment Certificates. **Schwan, Fred.** BNR Press, Port Clinton, Ohio, 1981. Covers notes issued for use by military personnel stationed overseas from 1946 to 1973.

Paper Money of the United States. Friedberg, Robert. The Coin and Currency Institute, Inc., Clifton, N.J., 1986. Catalog listings, with numbering system that is used hobby-wide.

Standard Catalog of National Bank Notes. Hickman, John, and Oakes, Dean. Krause Publications, Iola, Wis., 1982. Lists 117,007 different national bank notes in catalog fashion, plus historical information.

Standard Handbook of Modern United States Paper Money. O'Donnell, Chuck. Krause Publications, Iola, Wis., 1982. For collectors of small-sized notes, with complete listings of all blocks and star blocks issued, varieties and quantities produced.

America's Currency 1789-1866. American Numismatic Society, New York, 1985. Examines paper money in the United States as issued by private issuers and local and state governments. Reprints papers presented at the 1985 Coinage of the Americas Conference.

Confederate and Southern States Currency. Criswell, Grover C. Grover C. Criswell's Publications, Florida, 1976. Covers all CSA issues, plus states issues of the Civil War.

The Early Paper Money of America. Newman, Eric P. Western Publishing Co., Racine, Wis., 1976. Covers all paper money issued by the Continental Congress, 13 original Colonies.

Society of Paper Money Collectors Wismer update series. The SPMC has published a series of catalogs of obsolete notes by state and territory. Books available from the SPMC include Rhode Island, Florida, Mississippi, Texas, Iowa, Minnesota, Alabama, Maine, Indiana, New Jersey, Vermont, Arkansas, Pennsylvania and a volume covering the Indian Territory, Oklahoma and Kansas.

Joining a club

6

Belonging to your local coin club can put you in touch with people in your community with a mutual interest in one or more areas of numismatics.

Many collectors belong not only to local coin clubs, but also to state or regional coin clubs, associations devoted to a special collecting interests, the American Numismatic Association or international associations.

The question you might initially ask is, "Why do I need a club in the first place?"

Although many coin collectors are satisfied by pursuing the hobby alone, you may find it helpful and enjoyable sharing your experiences and knowledge at a local coin club meeting.

Collectors who have never belonged to a coin club before and beginning collectors may not even know a local coin club exists. Often, the local club will run a notice in the local newspaper announcing the date, time and location of its meetings.

Providing educational programs is the primary purpose of most clubs. Most of the programs are offered by the members

Joining a club gives you access to other collectors' experience and knowledge.

themselves. In some instances, an experienced collector may be paired with a newcomer to coordinate a program, expanding everyone's knowledge.

Some clubs present programs using slide presentations and scripts prepared by members or slide/script programs prepared by numismatic organizations such as the American Numismatic Association, the Token and Medal Society and the Civil War Token Society.

Local clubs often conduct a coin auction after the meeting's regular program has been completed. In most cases, the coins and other numismatic items offered for sale have been consigned or donated to the sale by the members. Depending on the size and geographic location of the club, the club may conduct one or more coin shows a year.

Clubs may also publish a bulletin or

newsletter informing members of numismatic news and events. Such publications may also list the club's program schedule and recap activities from previous meetings.

Of some 2,000 clubs in the United States, probably no two are operated alike or have the same programs.

The *Coin World* Club Center maintains information about many active clubs. Clubs wishing information about administration of a coin club can request secretary guidelines for keeping minutes, report forms, publicity outlines and membership cards.

Club presidents may request reprints for program aids, cards requesting samples of *Coin World*, information about fundraising projects, and a variety of literature to hand out at coin shows or conventions.

Collectors can pick up tips from other collectors about how to put together a winning coin exhibit at a local, regional or national coin show or convention. Many collectors enjoy competing for the plaques, trophies and ribbons in exhibit competitions. Other collectors enjoy putting together non-competitive exhibits just to show what can be done.

Clubs planning coin shows may ask to be listed in the *Coin World* show calendar and for help in resolving conflicting dates with other clubs holding shows in their areas.

Collectors planning to visit or move to another city may inquire about the meeting dates and locations of coin clubs in that area.

All these services are available by writing Club Center, *Coin World*, Box 150,

EVEN BEGINNING COLLECTORS may have interesting stories to tell other club members.

The American Numismatic Association supports many club activities throughout the country.

Sidney, Ohio 45365, telephone (513) 498-0800, ext. 242.

With roughly 30,000 members, the American Numismatic Association, referred to simply as the "ANA," is the world's largest numismatic organization. Now based in Colorado Springs, Colo., the ANA has its roots in Chicago.

In 1891, Dr. George Heath, publisher of *The Numismatist* (now the official ANA monthly magazine), announced in the August issue of that year that a group of numismatists meeting in Chicago felt a need for an association. The ANA was born two months later.

ANA headquarters boasts a museum, which displays, on a rotating basis, exhibits consisting of numismatic items loaned or donated to the ANA.

The ANA Library, which began with two books, now boasts several thousand books, volumes, special catalogs and periodicals.

All material, with the exception of the library's collection of rare books and catalogs, may be borrowed by ANA members. Reprints of articles that have appeared in *The Numismatist* can also be requested.

The association maintains an audio-visual education program for clubs, a coin authentication and grading service, programs for young numismatists, numismatic training seminars and sponsors an annual National Coin Week program designed to promote numismatics.

The association also has a representative program that links representatives of individual clubs with a regional coordinator.

For information about the ANA, write American Numismatic Association, 818 N. Cascade Ave., Colorado Springs, Colo. 80903; telephone (719) 632-2646.

Other national and regional coin associations, token and exonumia collectors organizations, organizations for paper money collectors and state associations:

Active Token Collectors Organization, 7411 Edledale Lane, Omaha, Neb. 68112.

Alabama Numismatic Society, Box 3601, West End Station, Birmingham, Ala. 35211.

American Medallic Sculpture Association, 431 Buena Vista Road, New City, N.Y. 10956.

American Numismatic Society, Broadway at 155th Street, New York, N.Y. 10032.

American Political Items Collectors, Box 340339, San Antonio, Texas, 78234.

American Society of Check Collectors, Route 2, Box 1, Iola, Wis. 54945.

American Tax Token Society, 7512 NE Bothell Way, #127, Bothell, Wash. 98011.

American Vecturist Association, 46 Fenwood Drive, Old Saybrook, Conn. 06475.

Amusement Token Collectors Association, 328 Avenue F, Redondo Beach, Calif. 90277.

Arkansas Numismatic Society, 6600 Baseline Road, Little Rock, Ark. 72209.

Bank Token Society, Box 383, Newtonville, Mass. 02160.

Blue Ridge Numismatic Association, 1501 Akins Drive, Chattanooga, Tenn. 37411.

Bond & Share Society, Box 120, Station K, Montreal, Quebec, Canada H1N 3K9.

Bust Nut Half Club, Box 4875, Margate, Fla. 33063.

California Association of Token Collectors, 516 W. 99th St., Los Angeles, Calif. 90044.

California Exonumist Society, Box 6599, San Diego, Calif. 92106.

California State Numismatic Association, Box 63, Upland, Calif. 91786.

Central States Numismatic Society, Box 223, Hiawatha, Iowa, 52233.

Civil War Token Society, Box 3412, Lake Mary, Fla. 32746.

Club of Illinois Numismatists, 2813 W. 85th Place, Chicago, Ill. 60652.

Colorado-Wyoming Numismatic Association, 519 W. Mountain Ave., Fort Collins, Colo. 80521.

Combined Organizations of Numismatic Error Collectors of America, Box 915, Palo Alto, Calif. 94302.

Currency Club of Chester County, Pa., 420 Owen Road, West Chester, Pa. 19380.

Dedicated Wooden Money Collectors, 1028 Azalea Court, La Marque, Texas 77568.

Early American Coppers, Box 15782, Cincinnati, Ohio 45215.

Empire State Numismatic Association, Rt. 2, Box 247, Troy, N.Y. 12182.

Essay Proof Society, Route 4, Colonial Drive, Katonah, N.Y. 10536.

Florida Token Society, Box 1091, Lake Alfred, Fla. 33850.

Florida United Numismatists, Box 2256, Clearwater, Fla. 34617.

Garden State Numismatic Association, Box 3462, Toms River, N.J. 08756.

Georgia Numismatic Association, Box 611, Lilburn, Ga. 30247.

Georgia State Token-Exonumia Association, Box 3412, Lake Mary, Fla. 32746.

Great Eastern Numismatic Association, 490 Green Hill Lane, Berwyn, Pa. 19312.

Hawaii State Numismatic Association, Box 477, Honolulu, Hawaii 96809.

Illinois Numismatic Association, 116 Cooper Drive, New Lenox, Ill. 60451.

Indiana State Numismatic Association, Box 44337, Indianapolis, Ind. 46204.

Indiana-Kentucky-Ohio Token & Medal Society, Box 192, Dayton, Ohio 45449.

International Bank Note Society, Box 1642, Racine, Wis. 53401.

International Organization of Wooden Money Collectors, Box 395, Goose Creek, S.C. 29445.

Iowa Numismatic Association, Box 65356, W. Des Moines, Iowa 50265.

John Reich Collectors Society, Box 205, Ypsilanti, Mich. 48197.

Kansas Numismatic Association, Rt. 3, Box 5, Chanute, Kan. 66720.

Kentucky State Numismatic Association, 1318 E. Breckinridge, Louisville, Ky. 40204.

Liberty Seated Collectors Club, Box 1062, Midland, Mich. 48641.

Louisiana Numismatic Society, Box 897, Opelousas, La. 70571.

Love Token Society, 3575 Sipler Lane, Huntington Valley, Pa. 19006.

Maine Numismatic Association, Box H, Brunswick, Maine 04011.

Maryland State Numismatic Association, Box 6533, Sparrows Point, Md. 21219.

Maryland Token & Medal Society, Box 3273, Baltimore, Md. 21228.

Michigan State Numismatic Society, Box 1157, Battle Creek, Mich. 49016.

Middle Atlantic Numismatic Association, Box 787, Pearl River, N.Y. 10965.

Midwest Numismatic Association, 9723 Marsh, Kansas City, Mo. 64134.

Minnesota Organization of Numismatists, Box 565, Rochester, Minn. 55903.

Mississippi Numismatic Association, Box 13525, Jackson, Miss. 39236.

Missouri Numismatic Society, 5005 S. Grand Blvd., St. Louis, Mo. 63111.

National Scrip Collectors Association, Box 29, Fayetteville, W. Va. 25840.

Nebraska Numismatic Association, Box 683, Sutherland, Neb. 69165.

New England Numismatic Association, Box 99, W. Roxbury, Mass. 02132.

New Hampshire Numismatic Association, Box 1655, Dover, N.H. 03820.

New Jersey Exonumia Society, Box 363, Cranford, N.J. 07016.

New Jersey Numismatic Society, Box 67, Wharton, N.J. 07885.

New York State Wooden Money Society, 25 N. Wayne Ave., West Haverstraw, N.Y. 10993.

North Carolina Numismatic Association, Box 20653, Greensboro, N.C. 27420.

Northern California Numismatic Association, Box 4104, Vallejo, Calif. 94590.

Numismatic Association of Southern California, Box 5173, Buena Park, Calif. 90622.

Numismatic Bibliomania Society, 4223 Iraquis, Lakewood, Calif. 90713.

Numismatists of Wisconsin, Box 155, Mazomanie, Wis. 53560.

Oklahoma Numismatic Association, Box 18753, Oklahoma City, Okla. 73154.

Old Timer Assay Commission Society, 3070 S. Franklin, Denver, Colo. 80210.

Oregon Numismatic Society, 4144 S.E. Clinton, Portland, Ore. 97202.

Pacific Coast Numismatic Society, 610 Arlington Ave., Berkeley, Calif. 94707.

Pacific Northwest Numismatic Association, 20121 1st Ave. S., Seattle, Wash. 98198.

Paper Money Collectors of Michigan, Box 163, Victor, N.Y. 14564.

Penn-Ohio Coin Clubs, 612 White St., Toledo, Ohio 43605.

Pennsylvania Association of Numismatists, Box 144, Pittsburgh, Pa. 15230.

Society for U.S. Commemorative Coins, 14252 Culver, Apt. 490, Irvine, Calif. 92714.

Society of Bearded Numismatists, Box 970218, Miama, Fla. 33197.

Society of Lincoln Cent Collectors, Box 5465, N. Hollywood, Calif. 91616.

Society of Paper Money Collectors, Box 1085, Florissant, Mo. 63031.

Society of Philatelists and Numismatists, 1929 Millis St., Montebello, Calif. 90640.

Society of Ration Token Collectors, Box J, Baltimore, Md. 21228.

South Carolina Numismatic Association, Box 12163, Columbia, S.C.

South Dakota Coin & Stamp Association, 106 W. 5th, Pierre, S.D. 57501.

Souvenir Card Collectors Society, Box 4155, Tulsa, Okla. 74159.

Tennessee State Numismatic Society, Box 80052, Chattanooga, Tenn. 37411.

Texas Numismatic Association, 2901 Silverleaf Drive, Austin, Texas 78757.

The Elongated Collectors, Box 161, Fenton, Mich. 48430.

Token and Medal Society, Box 3412, Lake Mary, Fla. 32746.

Utah Numismatic Society, Box 15054, Salt Lake City, Utah 84115.

Virginia Numismatic Association, 3902 Rose Lane, Annandale, Va. 22003.

World's Fair Collectors Society, Box 20806, Sarasota, Fla. 34238.

Guide to terms

7

Following are definitions of terms that appear in **bold type** throughout the preceding sections. Following each description is a reference to the page or pages where the term appears with the most meaningful context. Capitalization of some terms in numismatics may affect their meaning. The following are capitalized according to the style adopted by *Coin World*.

8 reales — Spanish silver coin popular at the time of American Independence, it was the model for the American silver dollar. These coins are sometimes associated with pirate treasures, and may be referred to as "pieces of eight." *Page 28*

About Good — Grading term. *Page 60*

About Uncirculated — Grading term. *Page 59*

altered coin — A coin that has been tampered with, usually in an attempt to make it appear rare or valuable. *Page 53*

annealing — A process of controlled heating and cooling of metal, annealing softens planchets for striking. *Page 34*

anvil die — In modern coin production, this is the bottom die, or the die fixed in position. The term is derived from the early days of coinage, when lumps of metal were placed on an anvil and struck with a hammer. *Page 30*

assay — To determine the precious metal content of a metal ore or alloy. *Page 32*

barter — Trade, especially trading goods or services for other goods or services in the absence of money. *Page 23*

bit — In Colonial America, the Spanish silver 8 reales coin was popular. This coin was sometimes cut into eight pieces for small change. Each piece was called a bit. When the United States modeled its silver dollar on the 8 reales, a bit referred to one-eighth of a dollar, or 12-1/2 cents. *Page 28*

bourse — Rhymes with "horse." At a coin show or convention, the bourse is the area where dealers set up tables of collectibles to sell. *Page 17*

circulate, circulation — The movement of money in an economy. Money is passed from person to person. Circulating coins are distinct from coins produced for collectors or investors. *Page 24*

clad coins — Generally refers to United States dime, quarter dollar, half dollar and dollar coins produced since 1965. These have layers of silver-colored copper-nickel bonded to a copper core. Clad coins replaced expensive silver coins in circulation. Other materials may be used for clad coins. *Page 11, 30*

coining press — The machine used to impress the image on pieces of metal to make coins. The coining press is one step of a long process in coin production. *Page 36*

collar — A ring of metal that contains the coin being struck in the coining press. The collar prevents metal from squeezing out from between the dies, and also may be used to place simple designs, such as reeding, on a coin's edge. *Page 37*

color — When coin collectors refer to a coin's color, they are refering to how it compares to its original appearance. Copper cents, for instance, when new are referred to as "red." When they age, they may become "brown." *Page 49*

commemorative coins — Coins struck to honor a person, event or place. These are usually produced in limited quantities for collectors, but they may also be placed into circulation, like the Bicentennial of American Independence quarter dollars, half dollars and dollars dated 1776-1976. *Page 18*

contact mark — Sometimes called a "bag mark," a contact mark is a scar or blemish on the surface of a coin. These are caused by normal handling of coins even before they reach circulation. *Page 46*

counterfeit — Counterfeits may be coins or paper money. They are produced with the intent to deceive or defraud. Some counterfeits are made to pass as circulating money, while others are intended to appear as valuable rarities. *Page 53*

debased — Money that becomes less valuable. When precious metals such as gold and silver were used in coins, over time, less pure metal was used in coins of the same denomination. The coins would buy less, because they were worth less. *Page 25*

die — A metal punch that impresses an image onto the surface of a coin. *Page 35*

dipped, dipping — Cleaning coins by placing them into a solvent. Dipping usually dissolves some of the coin's surface, making it artificially bright, but lacking in eye appeal. *Page 50, 66*

edge — The edge is the part of the coin that separates the obverse from the reverse. It can be smooth or may have some design. It is best to hold coins in your collection by the edge. *Page 5*

encapsulated coin — A coin that has been sealed into a plastic holder, usually after it has been graded by a grading service. *Page 52*

Extremely Fine — Grading term. *Page 59, 60*

eye appeal — The quality that makes a coin attractive. The precise definition of eye appeal differs with each individual. *Page 50*

face value — The value that is expressed on a piece of money, or its intended value by the issuer, such as "quarter dollar," "one cent," or "10 dollars." *Page 25*

fiat — A currency, or money system, that is not backed by precious metal reserves. *Page 27*

Fine — Grading term. *Page 59, 61*

Fleur de Coin — Grading term. *Page 61*

flip — A coin holder, usually a plastic one that has two pouches, one to hold a coin and the other to hold identification of the piece. It is folded over, or "flipped," to close. *Page 67*

flow lines — Microscopic lines in the surface metal of a coin. As light is reflected off flow lines, it produces a soft glow known as luster. Coins that are circulated or that have been harshly cleaned have their flow lines removed, and therefore little luster. *Page 47*

Fugio cents — The first coinage authorized by the new United States government in 1787. They were privately struck, but under federal inspection. *Page 29*

Good — Grading term. *Page 60, 61*

grade, grading — Grading is the act of determining the condition of a coin or other collectible. The grade is a number or phrase representative of the condition. *Page 45*

grading service — An organization that assigns grades to collectible items, usually for a fee. *Page 51*

half disme — Pronounced "half deem," this 1792 silver coin with a face value of 5 cents is believed to be the first coinage struck by the United States Mint. *Page 29*

hammer die — In modern coin production, it is the die that moves in the coining press. It is derived from the days when coinage was struck with a hammer. *Page 30*

hammer price — In an auction, this is the price the auctioneer calls the winning bid. The hammer price does not include buyer's fees or any other additional charges that the buyer may eventually pay for an auction lot. *Page 16*

hologram — A three-dimensional image. Some countries are experimenting with using holograms in their paper money as a security measure against counterfeiting. *Page 44*

hub — A positive-image metal punch used to make mirror-image dies. *Page 35.*

inflation, inflationary — In economics, when the same amount of money buys less over time. Inflation is why a car cost $3,000 in 1968, while a comparable car costs $10,000 in 1988. *Page 26*

intaglio — Intaglio is a method of printing that involves engraved metal plates. The paper is forced under high pressure into the ink-filled engraved lines of the plate. United States Federal Reserve notes are printed by the intaglio method as a measure against counterfeiting. *Page 41*

intrinsic value — The value of a coin's metal content, regardless of its face value. *Page 25*

legal tender — Money that has the official approval of a governing body. *Page 27*

legal tender bullion coin — Government-issued precious metal coins produced for investors, they have legal tender status, and usually a nominal face value, even though they are not intended to circulate as currency. *Page 27*

luster — The soft glow of a well-preserved coin, luster is the result of light reflecting off of microscopic flow lines in the metal. *Page 47*

master die — A metal punch used to produce "working hubs," which are then used to produce "working dies." *Page 35*

master hub — A metal punch used to produce "master dies." *Page 35*

medals — Collectible numismatic items, usually made from metal, that are commemorative or artistic. Some medals are produced by methods similar to coin production. Some medals are official government issues, but are not legal tender. *Page 6*

Mediocre — Grading term. *Page 62*

Mint State — Grading term. *Page 45, 58*

New, Uncirculated — Paper money grading term. *Page 60*

numismatics, numismatist — The broad term covering the study of money or money-like items. A numismatist is more deeply involved in research and study than a "collector." *Page 5*

obsolete paper money — Paper money issued prior to 1865 by banks that are no longer operating. The term "broken bank note" will sometimes be used, although not all banks that issued these notes closed because of failure. *Page 10*

obverse — On coins, the front or face; "heads." Usually the side with the dominant design. *Page 5*

overprinting — In the production of United States Federal Reserve notes, the main designs are printed on the face and back. Then the serial numbers and Federal Reserve seals are "overprinted" in a separate process. *Page 42*

paper money — Printed monetary instruments. Modern collectors may be challenged for a new term as nations experiment with plastics and other materials for their printed money. Some collectors incorrectly use the term "bank notes" to refer to all paper money, or the term "currency" to refer to only paper money. Currency may also be coin. *Page 26*

patina — The surface quality that a coin acquires over time as the metal reacts with the environment. *Page 65*

planchet — Sometimes called a blank or flan, it is a piece of metal formed and ready to be struck into coinage, but not yet impressed with the coin design. *Page 33*

polyvinylchloride, PVC — A chemical found in some soft, pliable plastic coin or paper money holders. PVC degrades into a particularly ugly and damaging goo. Storage devices containing PVC should be avoided. *Page 68*

Poor — Grading term. *Page 62*

Proof — Sometimes used as a grading term, especially with a number, such as "Proof 65." Technically, it is a method of manufacture using great care to produce special collectibles. In paper money circles, a proof (lowercase p) is a test printing before a production run. *Page 58*

Proof set — Generally a representative sample of the coins produced by a nation for circulation, but manufactured and packaged specifically for collectors. Some Proof sets may be privately assembled and packaged. *Page 20*

reeding — The ridges on the edge of a coin. *Page 37*

replica — A copy or reproduction of a numismatic item. *Page 54*

reverse — The back of a coin; "tails." Usually the secondary design side. *Page 5*

riddlers — Vibrating screens that sort out non-standard planchets. *Page 33*

rim — The raised ridge around the obverse and reverse of a coin. The rim's function is to protect the surface and help in stacking. The term is sometimes confused with "edge." *Page 35*

screw press — Early hand-operated machine for striking coins. The operator swung a weighted arm that turned a screw, which then pressed the die into the planchet. More accurate than hand-hammering. *Page 30*

silver certificates — Paper money issued by the United States, they could be redeemed for silver until the mid-1960s. No longer produced, they are still legal tender, but cannot be redeemed for silver. *Page 27*

slab — Popular nickname for certain kinds of coin encapsulation methods, especially those that are permanently sealed and rectangular. *Page 52, 69*

souvenir cards — Popular collectible items, souvenir cards are usually well-printed on heavy paper using an engraving used on paper money. They also contain some information of a historic or commemorative nature. *Page 6*

specie — Usually precious metal coins in circulation valued at their precious metal content. Paper money that can be redeemed in coin is specie currency. *Page 27*

strike — The act of impressing the image of a die into a planchet, making a coin. The quality of strike is important when determining a coin's condition and value. *Page 48*

strip — Rolls of coinage metal to be punched into planchets. *Page 32*

surcharge — An extra charge placed on an item, the revenue from a surcharge is usually earmarked for a specific fund. It has been the recent practice of the United States Congress to place a surcharge on commemorative coins either to benefit a worthy organization, or to be used to reduce the national debt. *Page 18*

tokens — Coin-like money substitutes, generally privately issued. Tokens have played an important part in the economy of the United States during periods when small change was difficult to obtain. *Page 6*

toning — As the metal in a coin reacts with its environment, it may produce varying shades of color. Toning can be very attractive or very ugly. How it affects the value of a coin is a matter of personal taste. *Page 49*

Uncirculated — Technically, a coin or note that has never been used. Grading term. *Page 45, 58, 60*

Uncirculated Mint set — Usually a representative set of a nation's circulating coinage that has been specially packaged for collectors, but not so elaborate as a Proof set. *Page 19*

upsetting mill — A machine that squeezes planchets so that they have a raised rim, in preparation for striking into coins. *Page 34*

Very Fine — Grading term. *Page 59, 61*

Very Good — Grading term. *Page 59, 61*

vignettes — Small scenes engraved on paper money. Sometimes produced for collectors as "vignette sheets." The term derives from the fact that many scenes on paper money are details of larger paintings. *Page 6*

watermark — When paper is manufactured, it is possible to slightly vary the thickness in certain areas and produce a design. These designs will appear as shadowy when the paper is held up to the light. It is useful in paper money as a security measure against counterfeiting. *Page 44*

Wheat Ear cent — Lincoln cent produced from 1909-1958, the name comes from the two stalks of wheat on the reverse of the coins. *Page 11*

working die — A metal punch that is used to impress images into coins. *Page 36*

working hub — A metal punch used to produce "working dies." *Page 36*

Using the checklist

8

The checklist of United States coins that makes up the balance of this book has a number of uses for the beginning collector.

✓ It can be used as a record-keeper of coins in your collection.
✓ It can be used as a list of coins you want to purchase.
✓ It can be used as a first reference, for visual identification of coins.
✓ It can be used to determine mintages of U.S. coins.

The checklist is organized by denomination, type and date. The denomination is the face value of the coin. The list begins with half cents and runs through American Eagle bullion coins.

Within each denomination are types. These are the main design styles of a coin series. Finally, the coins are listed by date and Mint of manufacture.

For the current series — the Lincoln cent, Jefferson 5 cents, Roosevelt dime, Washington quarter, Kennedy half, the modern commemoratives, American Eagle bullion coins, and Proof and Uncirculated sets — room has been allowed for future issues. The dates and Mint marks listed beyond 1989 are those that are most probable for the Mint to issue. There may be changes, however.

A word about mintages — the mintages shown here for each coin are derived from a variety of sources. The numbers represent the quantity of coins originally produced — not necessarily the number surviving today. Silver coins in particular were vulnerable to meltdowns. When the price of silver bullion gets high enough, many people melt their coins for their silver content.

Where an "(R)" appears under the mintage column, a significant number of the pieces are restrikes. Where an (R) follows a number, the number represents the original mintage.

Rarity is based on the number of coins that survive, and the frequency with which they appear for sale.

Value is based on supply and demand. For a guide to the value of individual coins, refer to a price guide such as the *Coin World Guide to U.S. Coins, Prices & Value Trends* or the Trends section of the weekly *Coin World* newspaper. Coin values can change very quickly, and it is necessary to know the condition of the coin to determine its value.

Each listing in the checklist has four information blocks: grade, date purchased, amount paid and comments (you might want to list the dealer you obtained the coin from, for example).

Not all varieties of U.S. coins are listed. Those included are the ones deemed most popular among collectors. Several popular error coins are included, such as the 1955 Doubled Die Lincoln cent.

In a number of cases, no business strikes were issued in a particular year, although Proof coins were struck. In these cases, the word "Proof" follows the date, and the mintage figure is the number of Proof coins struck. When the word "Proof" does not appear, the mintage figure represents the number of business strikes, although Proof coins may also have been struck. Modern Proof coins and sets are included, as are all commemorative coins from the 1892 Columbian Exposition half dollar to the planned 1990 silver dollar commemorating the centennial of President Eisenhower's birth. Proof coins from 1936-1995 are also listed separately by denomination, even though Proof coins from 1950-1989 (and projecting into 1995) were sold by the Mint in sets only. In addition, the inclusion of Proof "sets" for the years 1936-1942 is not meant to imply the sets were official. The coins were sold individually; the "set" mintage represents the lowest Proof mintage of the denominations of that year, the theoretical limit to the number of complete Proof sets that could have been assembled. Also listed are the American Eagle bullion coins, Proofs and business strikes, issued since 1986.

Contents of the checklist

Abbreviation key

1st HS — First Hair Style	MD — Medium Date
2nd HS — Second Hair Style	NM — No Motto
Arr. — Arrows	Obv. — Obverse
Cl. — Closed	Pl. Edge — Plain Edge
Dbl. — Double	Pl. 4 — Plain 4
Dr. Bust — Draped Bust	Rev. — Reverse
Her. Eagle — Heraldic Eagle	SD — Small Date
Hor. — Horizontal	SL — Small Letters
Inv. — Inverted	Sl 5, Knb — Slanting 5, Knob on Ear
LD — Large Date	S of A — States of America
Lg. — Large	Spiked — Spiked Chin
LL — Large Letters	TF — Tail Feathers
LM — Large Motto	Vars. — Varieties

Half cent Liberty Cap, Left

	Mintage	Grade	Date purchased	Amount paid	Comments
1793..................	35,334				

Half cent Liberty Cap, Right

	Mintage	Grade	Date purchased	Amount paid	Comments
1794..................	81,600				
1795..................	139,690				
1796 With Pole ..	1,390				
1796 No Pole.....	Incl. above				
1797 Plain Edge	127,840				
1797 Lettered Edge	Incl. above				
1797 Gripped Edge	Incl. above				

Half cent Draped Bust

	Mintage	Grade	Date purchased	Amount paid	Comments
1800	202,908				
1802/0	20,266				
1802/0 rev of 1800	Incl. above				
1803	92,000				
1804	1,055,312				
1804 Spiked	Incl. above				
1805	814,464				
1805 Small 5, Stars	Incl. above				
1806	356,000				
1806 Small 6, Stars	Incl. above				
1807	476,000				
1808	400,000				
1808/7	Incl. above				

Half cent Classic Head

	Mintage	Grade	Date purchased	Amount paid	Comments
1809	1,154,572				
1809/6	Incl. above				
1810	215,000				

Cent Classic Head (continued)

	Mintage	Grade	Date purchased	Amount paid	Comments
1811...................	63,140				
1825...................	63,000				
1826...................	234,000				
1828 13 Stars	606,000				
1828 12 Stars	Incl. above				
1829...................	487,000				
1831...................	2,200(R)				
1832...................	154,000				
1833...................	120,000				
1834...................	141,000				
1835...................	398,000				
1836 Proof.	(R)				
1840 Proof.	(R)				
1841 Proof	(R)				
1842 Proof.	(R)				
1843 Proof.	(R)				
1844 Proof.	(R)				
1845 Proof.	(R)				
1846 Proof.	(R)				
1847 Proof.	(R)				
1848 Proof.	(R)				
1849 Proof.	(R)				

Half cent Coronet

	Mintage	Grade	Date purchased	Amount paid	Comments
1849 Large Date	43,364				
1850...................	39,812				
1851...................	147,672				

Cent Coronet (continued)

	Mintage	Grade	Date purchased	Amount paid	Comments
1852 Proof.........	(R)				
1853	129,694				
1854	55,358				
1855	56,500				
1856	40,430				
1857	35,180				

Cent Flowing Hair, Chain or Wreath

	Mintage	Grade	Date purchased	Amount paid	Comments
1793 Chain, AMERICA	36,103				
1793 AMERI	Incl. above				
1793 Wreath	63,353				
1793 Lettered Edge	Incl. above				

Cent Liberty Cap

	Mintage	Grade	Date purchased	Amount paid	Comments
1793...................	11,056				
1794 Head of '93	918,521				
1794...................	Incl. above				
1794 Starred......	Incl. above				
1795 Plain Edge	538,500				
1795 Lettered Edge	Incl. above				
1795 Jefferson Head, ... Plain Edge.......	Incl. above				
1796...................	109,825				

Cent Draped Bust

	Mintage	Grade	Date purchased	Amount paid	Comments
1796 Reverse of 1794	363,375				
1796 Reverse of 1796	Incl. above				

Cent Draped Bust (continued)

	Mintage	Grade	Date purchased	Amount paid	Comments
1796 Reverse of 1797...............	Incl. above				
1796 LIHERTY	Incl. above				
1797 Rev. of 1797, Stars...............	897,510				
1797 Gripped Edge '96.........	Incl. above				
1797 Plain Edge '96...................	Incl. above				
1797 Rev '97, Stemless.........	Incl. above				
1798 1st Hair Style	1,841,745				
1798 2nd Hair Style...............	Incl. above				
1798 Rev '96......	Incl. above				
1798/7 1st Hair Style................	Incl. above				
1799	42,540				
1799/8	Incl. above				
1800 Normal Date	2,822,175				
1800/1798 1st HS	Incl. above				
1800 80/79 2nd HS	Incl. above				
1801	1,362,837				
1801 3 Errors.......	Incl. above				
1801 1/000.........	Incl. above				
1801 1/100 over 1/000	Incl. above				
1802	3,435,100				
1802 Stemless....	Incl. above				
1802 1/000.........	Incl. above				
1803	3,131,691				
1803 LD, Small Fraction..........	Incl. above				
1803 LD, Large Fraction..........	Incl. above				
1803 Stemless....	Incl. above				
1803 1/100 over 1/000	Incl. above				
1804	96,500				
1805	941,116				
1806	348,000				
1807 Large Fraction..........	829,221				
1807 Small Fraction..........	Incl. above				

Cent Draped Bust (continued)

	Mintage	Grade	Date purchased	Amount paid	Comments
1807/6 Large 7..	Incl. above				
1807/6 Small 7...	Incl. above				

Cent Classic Head

	Mintage	Grade	Date purchased	Amount paid	Comments
1808	1,007,000				
1809	222,867				
1810	1,458,500				
1810 10/09	Incl. above				
1811	218,025				
1811/0	Incl. above				
1812	1,075,500				
1813	418,000				
1814	357,830				

Cent Coronet

	Mintage	Grade	Date purchased	Amount paid	Comments
1816	2,820,982				
1817 13 Stars	3,948,400				
1817 15 Stars	Incl. above				
1818	3,167,000				
1819	2,671,000				
1819/8	Incl. above				
1820	4,407,550				
1820/19	Incl. above				
1821	389,000				
1822	2,072,339				
1823	68,061				
1823/2	Incl. above				
1824	1,193,939				
1824/2	Incl. above				
1825	1,461,100				
1826	1,517,425				
1826/5	Incl. above				
1827	2,357,732				
1828 LD	2,260,624				
1828 SD	Incl. above				
1829 Lg. Letters	1,414,500				
1829 Md. Letters	Incl. above				
1830 Lg. Letters	1,711,500				
1830 Md. Letters	Incl. above				
1831	3,539,260				
1832	2,362,000				
1833	2,739,000				
1834	1,855,100				

Cent Coronet (continued)

	Mintage	Grade	Date purchased	Amount paid	Comments
1834 Lg. 8, Stars, rev. Letters	Incl. above				
1834 Lg. 8, Stars, Md. Letters	Incl. above				
1835....................	3,878,400				
1835 Type 36	Incl. above				
1836....................	2,111,000				
1837....................	5,558,300				
1838....................	6,370,200				
1839 Head of '38	Incl. above				
1839/6	3,128,661				
1839 Silly Head..	Incl. above				
1839 Booby Head	Incl. above				
1839....................	Incl. above				
1840....................	2,462,700				
1840 SD, Lg. 18..	Incl. above				
1841 SD.............	1,597,367				
1842....................	2,383,390				
1843 Petite Sm Letters...........	2,425,342				
1843 Mature Lg Letters...........	Incl. above				
1843 Petite Lg Letters...........	Incl. above				
1844....................	2,398,752				
1844/81..............	Incl. above				
1845....................	3,894,804				
1846....................	4,120,800				
1846 SD.............	Incl. above				
1847....................	6,183,669				
1847 7/Sm 7	Incl. above				
1848....................	6,415,799				
1849....................	4,178,500				
1850....................	4,426,844				
1851....................	9,889,707				
1851/81..............	Incl. above				
1852....................	5,063,094				
1853....................	6,641,131				
1854....................	4,236,156				
1855....................	1,574,829				

Cent Coronet (continued)

	Mintage	Grade	Date purchased	Amount paid	Comments
1855 Slant 5, Knob	Incl. above				
1856	2,690,463				
1857 Sm. Date ..	333,456				
1857 Lg. Date....	Incl. above				

Cent Flying Eagle

	Mintage	Grade	Date purchased	Amount paid	Comments
1856	(Pattern)				
1857	17,450,000				
1858 Large Letters	24,600,000				
1858 Small Letters	Incl. above				
1858/7	Incl. above				

Cent Indian Head

	Mintage	Grade	Date purchased	Amount paid	Comments
1859	36,400,000				
1860 Shield added............	20,566,000				
1861	10,100,000				
1862	28,075,000				
1863	49,840,000				

Cent **Indian Head (continued)**

	Mintage	Grade	Date purchased	Amount paid	Comments
1864 copper-nickel.	13,740,000				
1864 bronze.	39,233,714				
1864 bronze, Initial L............	Incl. above				
1865....................	35,429,286				
1866....................	9,826,000				
1867....................	9,821,000				
1868....................	10,266,500				
1869....................	6,420,000				
1869/9	Incl. above				
1870....................	5,275,000				
1871....................	3,929,500				
1872....................	4,042,000				
1873 Open 3.....	11,676,500				
1873 Closed 3...	Incl. above				
1873 Doubled LIBERTY	Incl. above				
1874....................	14,187,500				
1875....................	13,528,000				
1876....................	7,944,000				
1877....................	852,000				
1878....................	5,797,500				
1879....................	16,228,000				
1880....................	38,961,000				
1881....................	39,208,000				
1882....................	38,578,000				
1883....................	45,591,500				
1884....................	23,257,800				
1885....................	11,761,594				
1886....................	17,650,000				
1887....................	45,223,523				
1888....................	37,489,832				
1888/7	Incl. above				
1889....................	48,866,025				
1890....................	57,180,114				
1891....................	47,070,000				
1892....................	37,647,087				
1893....................	46,640,000				
1894....................	16,749,500				

Cent Indian Head (continued)

	Mintage	Grade	Date purchased	Amount paid	Comments
1895	38,341,574				
1896	39,055,431				
1897	50,464,392				
1898	49,821,284				
1899	53,598,000				
1900	66,821,284				
1901	79,609,158				
1902	87,374,704				
1903	85,092,703				
1904	61,326,198				
1905	80,717,011				
1906	96,020,530				
1907	108,137,143				
1908	32,326,367				
1908-S	1,115,000				
1909	14,368,470				
1909-S	309,000				

Cent Lincoln, Wheat Ears or Memorial

	Mintage	Grade	Date purchased	Amount paid	Comments
1909 VDB	27,994,580				
1909-S VDB	484,000				
1909	72,700,420				
1909-S	1,825,000				
1910	146,798,813				
1910-S	6,045,000				
1911	101,176,054				
1911-D	12,672,000				

Cent Lincoln, Wheat Ears (continued)

	Mintage	Grade	Date purchased	Amount paid	Comments
1911-S	4,026,000				
1912	68,150,915				
1912-D	10,411,000				
1912-S	4,431,000				
1913	76,529,504				
1913-D	15,804,000				
1913-S	6,101,000				
1914	75,237,067				
1914-D	1,193,000				
1914-S	4,137,000				
1915	29,090,970				
1915-D	22,050,000				
1915-S	4,833,000				
1916	131,832,627				
1916-D	35,956,000				
1916-S	22,510,000				
1917	196,429,785				
1917-D	55,120,000				
1917-S	32,620,000				
1918	288,104,634				
1918-D	47,830,000				
1918-S	34,680,000				
1919	392,021,000				
1919-D	57,154,000				
1919-S	139,760,000				
1920	310,165,000				
1920-D	49,280,000				
1920-S	46,220,000				
1921	39,157,000				
1921-S	15,274,000				
1922-D	7,160,000				
1922 Plain	Incl. above				
1923	74,723,000				
1923-S	8,700,000				
1924	75,178,000				
1924-D	2,520,000				
1924-S	11,696,000				
1925	139,949,000				
1925-D	22,580,000				

Cent Lincoln, Wheat Ears (continued)

	Mintage	Grade	Date purchased	Amount paid	Comments
1925-S	26,380,000				
1926	157,088,000				
1926-D...............	28,020,000				
1926-S	4,550,000				
1927	144,440,000				
1927-D...............	27,170,000				
1927-S	14,276,000				
1928	134,116,000				
1928-D...............	31,170,000				
1928-S	17,266,000				
1929	185,262,000				
1929-D...............	41,730,000				
1929-S	50,148,000				
1930	157,415,000				
1930-D...............	40,100,000				
1930-S	24,286,000				
1931	19,396,000				
1931-D...............	4,480,000				
1931-S	866,000				
1932	9,062,000				
1932-D...............	10,500,000				
1933	14,360,000				
1933-D...............	6,200,000				
1934	219,080,000				
1934-D...............	28,446,000				
1935	245,388,000				
1935-D...............	47,000,000				
1935-S	38,702,000				
1936	309,632,000				
1936-D...............	40,620,000				
1936-S	29,130,000				
1936 Proof.	5,569				
1937	309,170,000				
1937-D...............	50,430,000				
1937-S	34,500,000				
1937 Proof.	9,320				
1938	156,682,000				
1938-D...............	20,010,000				
1938-S	15,180,000				

Cent Lincoln, Wheat Ears (continued)

	Mintage	Grade	Date purchased	Amount paid	Comments
1938 Proof.	14,734				
1939....................	316,466,000				
1939-D	15,160,000				
1939-S.................	52,070,000				
1939 Proof.	13,520				
1940....................	586,810,000				
1940-D	81,390,000				
1940-S.................	112,940,000				
1940 Proof.	15,872				
1941....................	887,018,000				
1941-D	128,700,000				
1941-S.................	92,460,000				
1941 Proof.	21,100				
1942....................	657,796,000				
1942-D	206,698,000				
1942-S.................	85,590,000				
1942 Proof.	32,600				
1943....................	684,628,670				
1943-D	217,660,000				
1943-S.................	191,550,000				
1944....................	1,435,400,000				
1944-D	430,578,000				
1944-D/S Variety 1	Incl. above				
1944-D/S Variety 2	Incl. above				
1944-S.................	282,760,000				
1945....................	1,040,515,000				
1945-D	226,268,000				
1945-S.................	181,770,000				
1946....................	991,655,000				
1946-D	315,690,000				
1946-S.................	198,100,000				
1947....................	190,555,000				
1947-D	194,750,000				
1947-S.................	99,000,000				
1948....................	317,570,000				
1948-D	172,630,500				
1948-S.................	81,735,000				
1949....................	217,775,000				
1949-D	153,132,500				

Cent Lincoln, Wheat Ears (continued)

	Mintage	Grade	Date purchased	Amount paid	Comments
1949-S	64,290,000				
1950	272,635,000				
1950 Proof	51,386				
1950-D	334,950,000				
1950-S	118,505,000				
1951	294,576,000				
1951 Proof	57,500				
1951-D	625,355,000				
1951-S	136,010,000				
1952	186,765,000				
1952 Proof	81,980				
1952-D	746,130,000				
1952-S	137,800,004				
1953	256,755,000				
1953 Proof	128,800				
1953-D	700,515,000				
1953-S	181,835,000				
1954	71,640,050				
1954 Proof	233,350				
1954-D	251,552,500				
1954-S	96,190,000				
1955	330,580,000				
1955 Proof	378,200				
1955 Doubled Die	Incl. above				
1955-D	563,257,500				
1955-S	44,610,000				
1956	420,745,000				
1956 Proof	669,384				
1956-D	1,098,210,100				
1957	282,540,000				
1957 Proof	1,247,952				
1957-D	1,051,342,000				
1958	252,525,000				
1958 Proof	875,652				
1958-D	800,953,300				
1959 Memorial reverse.	609,715,000				
1959 Proof	1,149,291				
1959-D	1,279,760,000				

Cent Lincoln, Memorial (continued)

	Mintage	Grade	Date purchased	Amount paid	Comments
1960 Large Date.	586,405,000				
1960 Small Date	Incl. above				
1960 Proof	1,691,602				
1960-D Large Date.	1,580,884,000				
1960-D Small Date..............	Incl. above				
1961....................	753,345,000				
1961 Proof	3,028,244				
1961-D.	1,753,266,700				
1962....................	606,045,000				
1962 Proof	3,218,019				
1962-D.	1,793,148,400				
1963....................	754,110,000				
1963 Proof	3,075,645				
1963-D.	1,774,020,400				
1964....................	2,648,575,000				
1964 Proof	3,950,762				
1964-D.	3,799,071,500				
1965....................	1,497,224,900				
1966....................	2,188,147,783				
1967....................	3,048,667,100				
1968....................	1,707,880,970				
1968-D.	2,886,269,600				
1968-S.	258,270,001				
1968-S Proof.	3,041,506				
1969....................	1,136,910,000				
1969-D.	4,002,832,200				
1969-S.	544,375,000				
1969-S Proof.	2,934,631				
1970....................	1,898,315,000				
1970-D.	2,891,438,900				
1970-S Large Date.	690,560,004				
1970-S Small Date	Incl. above				
1970-S Proof.	2,632,810				
1971....................	1,919,490,000				
1971-D...............	2,911,045,600				
1971-S................	525,130,054				
1971-S Proof.	3,220,733				

Cent Lincoln, Memorial (continued)

	Mintage	Grade	Date purchased	Amount paid	Comments
1972	2,933,255,000				
1972 Doubled Die	Incl. above				
1972-D	2,655,071,400				
1972-S	376,932,437				
1972-S Proof.	3,260,996				
1973	3,728,245,000				
1973-D	3,549,576,588				
1973-S	317,168,010				
1973-S Proof.	2,760,339				
1974	4,232,140,523				
1974-D	4,235,098,000				
1974-S	409,421,878				
1974-S Proof.	2,612,568				
1975	5,451,476,142				
1975-D	4,505,275,300				
1975-S Proof.	2,845,450				
1976	4,674,292,426				
1976-D	4,221,592,455				
1976-S Proof.	4,123,056				
1977	4,469,930,000				
1977-D	4,194,062,300				
1977-S Proof.	3,236,798				
1978	5,558,605,000				
1978-D	4,280,233,400				
1978-S Proof.	3,120,285				
1979	6,018,515,000				
1979-D	4,139,357,254				
1979-S Proof.	3,677,175				
1980	7,414,705,000				
1980-D	5,140,098,660				
1980-S Proof.	3,554,806				
1981	7,491,750,000				
1981-D	5,373,235,677				
1981-S Proof.	4,063,083				
1982 Large Date, copper.	10,712,525,000				
1982 Small Date, copper	Incl. above				
1982 Large Date, zinc	Incl. above				

Cent Lincoln, Memorial (continued)

	Mintage	Grade	Date purchased	Amount paid	Comments
1982 Small Date, zinc	Incl. above				
1982-D Large date, copper	6,012,979,368				
1982-D Large Date, zinc	Incl. above				
1982-D Small Date, zinc	Incl. above				
1982--S Proof	3,857,479				
1983	7,571,590,000				
1983 Doubled Die	Incl. above				
1983-D	6,467,199,428				
1983-S Proof	3,138,765				
1984	8,151,079,000				
1984 Doubled Die	Incl. above				
1984-D	5,569,238,906				
1984-S Proof	2,748,430				
1985	4,951,904,887				
1985-D	5,287,399,926				
1985-S Proof	3,362,821				
1986	4,491,395,493				
1986-D	4,442,866,698				
1986-S Proof	2,411,180				
1987	4,682,466,931				
1987-D	4,879,389,514				
1987-S Proof	3,715,041				
1988	6,092,810,000				
1988-D	5,253,740,443				
1988-S Proof					
1989					
1989-D					
1989-S Proof					
1990					
1990-D					
1990-S Proof					
1991					
1991-D					
1991-S Proof					
1992					
1992-D					
1992-S Proof					

Cent Lincoln, Memorial (continued)

	Mintage	Grade	Date purchased	Amount paid	Comments
1993					
1993-D					
1993-S Proof					
1994					
1994-D					
1994-S Proof					
1995					
1995-D					
1995-S Proof					

2 cents

	Mintage	Grade	Date purchased	Amount paid	Comments
1864 Small Motto	19,847,500				
1864 Large Motto	Incl. above				
1865	13,640,000				
1866	3,177,000				
1867	2,938,750				
1868	2,803,750				
1869	1,546,500				
1869/8	Incl. above				
1870	861,250				
1871	721,250				
1872	65,000				
1873 Proof	1,000(R)				

3 cents **copper-nickel**

	Mintage	Grade	Date purchased	Amount paid	Comments
1865..................	11,382,000				
1866..................	4,801,000				
1867..................	3,915,000				
1868..................	3,252,000				
1869..................	1,604,000				
1870..................	1,335,000				
1871..................	604,000				
1872..................	862,000				
1873 Open 3.....	1,173,000				
1873 Closed 3...	Incl. above				
1874..................	790,000				
1875..................	228,000				
1876..................	162,000				
1877 Proof.........	510				
1878 Proof.........	2,350				
1879..................	38,000				
1880..................	21,000				
1881..................	1,077,000				
1882..................	22,200				
1883..................	4,000				
1884..................	1,700				
1885..................	1,000				
1886 Proof.........	4,290				
1887..................	5,001				
1887/6 Proof......	Less than 2,960				
1888..................	36,501				
1889..................	18,125				

3 cents silver

	Mintage	Grade	Date purchased	Amount paid	Comments
1851	5,447,400				
1851-O	720,000				
1852	18,663,500				
1853	11,400,000				
1854	671,000				
1855	139,000				
1856	1,458,000				
1857	1,042,000				
1858	1,604,000				
1859	365,000				
1860	286,000				
1861	497,000				
1862	343,000				
1862/1	Incl. above				
1863	21,000				
1863/2	Incl. above				
1864	12,000				
1865	8,000				
1866	22,000				
1867	4,000				
1868	3,500				
1869	4,500				
1869/8	Incl. above				
1870	3,000				
1871	3,400				
1872	1,000				
1873 Proof	600				

5 cents Shield

	Mintage	Grade	Date purchased	Amount paid	Comments
1866 Rays..........	14,742,500				
1867 Rays..........	30,909,500				
1867 No Rays....	Incl. above				
1868..................	28,817,000				
1869..................	16,395,000				
1870..................	4,806,000				
1871..................	561,000				
1872..................	6,036,000				
1873 Open 3.....	4,550,000				
1873 Closed 3...	Incl. above				
1874..................	3,538,000				
1875..................	2,097,000				
1876..................	2,530,000				
1877 Proof.........	510				
1878 Proof.........	2,350				
1879..................	25,900				
1880..................	16,000				
1881..................	68,800				
1882..................	11,473,500				
1883..................	1,451,500				
1883/2	Incl. above				

5 cents Liberty Head

	Mintage	Grade	Date purchased	Amount paid	Comments
1883 No CENTS .	5,474,300				
1883 CENTS	16,026,200				
1884	11,270,000				
1885	1,472,700				
1886	3,326,000				
1887	15,260,692				
1888	10,715,901				
1889	15,878,025				
1890	16,256,532				
1891	16,832,000				
1892	11,696,897				
1893	13,368,000				
1894	5,410,500				
1895	9,977,822				
1896	8,841,058				
1897	20,426,797				
1898	12,539,292				
1899	26,027,000				
1900	27,253,733				
1901	26,478,228				
1902	31,478,561				
1903	28,004,935				
1904	21,401,350				
1905	29,825,125				
1906	38,612,000				
1907	39,213,325				
1908	22,684,557				
1909	11,585,763				
1910	30,166,948				
1911	39,557,639				

5 cents Liberty Head (continued)

	Mintage	Grade	Date purchased	Amount paid	Comments
1912...............	26,234,569				
1912-D.............	8,474,000				
1912-S.............	238,000				

5 cents Indian Head ("Buffalo")

	Mintage	Grade	Date purchased	Amount paid	Comments
1913 Bison on Mound...........	30,992,000				
1913-D Bison on Mound..........	5,337,000				
1913-S Bison on Mound..........	2,105,000				
1913 Bison on Plain..............	29,857,186				
1913-D Bison on Plain..............	4,156,000				
1913-S Bison on Plain..............	1,209,000				
1914..................	20,664,463				
1914-D..............	3,912,000				
1914-S..............	3,470,000				
1915..................	20,986,220				
1915-D..............	7,569,500				
1915-S..............	1,505,000				
1916..................	63,497,466				
1916 Doubled Die	Incl. above				
1916-D..............	13,333,000				
1916-S..............	11,860,000				
1917..................	51,424,029				
1917-D..............	9,910,800				
1917-S..............	4,193,000				
1918..................	32,086,314				

5 cents Indian Head (continued)

	Mintage	Grade	Date purchased	Amount paid	Comments
1918-D...............	8,362,000				
1918/17-D..........	Incl. above				
1918-S	4,882,000				
1919	60,868,000				
1919-D...............	8,006,000				
1919-S	7,521,000				
1920	63,093,000				
1920-D...............	9,418,000				
1920-S	9,689,000				
1921	10,633,000				
1921-S	1,557,000				
1923	35,715,000				
1923-S	6,142,000				
1924	21,620,000				
1924-D...............	5,258,000				
1924-S	1,437,000				
1925	35,565,100				
1925-D...............	4,450,000				
1925-S	6,286,000				
1926	44,693,000				
1926-D...............	5,638,000				
1926-S	970,000				
1927	37,981,000				
1927-D...............	5,730,000				
1927-S	3,430,000				
1928	23,411,000				
1928-D...............	6,436,000				
1928-S	6,936,000				
1929	36,446,000				
1929-D...............	8,370,000				
1929-S	7,754,000				
1930	22,849,000				
1930-S	5,435,000				
1931-S	1,200,000				
1934	20,213,003				
1934-D...............	7,480,000				
1935	58,264,000				
1935-D...............	12,092,000				
1935-S	10,300,000				

5 cents Indian Head (continued)

	Mintage	Grade	Date purchased	Amount paid	Comments
1936	118,997,000				
1936-D	24,814,000				
1936-S	14,930,000				
1936 Proof	4,420				
1937	79,480,000				
1937-D	17,826,000				
1937-D 3 Legs	Incl. above				
1937-S	5,635,000				
1937 Proof	5,769				
1938-D	7,020,000				
1938-D/S	Incl. above				
1938 Proof	19,365				

5 cents Jefferson

	Mintage	Grade	Date purchased	Amount paid	Comments
1938	19,496,000				
1938-D	5,376,000				
1938-S	4,105,000				
1939	120,615,000				
1939 Doubled Die	Incl. above				
1939-D	3,514,000				
1939-S	6,630,000				
1939 Proof	12,535				
1940	176,485,000				
1940-D	43,540,000				
1940-S	39,690,000				
1940 Proof	14,158				
1941	203,265,000				
1941-D	53,432,000				
1941-S	43,445,000				

5 cents Jefferson (continued)

	Mintage	Grade	Date purchased	Amount paid	Comments
1941 Proof	18,720				
1942	49,789,000				
1942-P	57,873,000				
1942-D	13,938,000				
1942-S	32,900,000				
1942 Proof	57,200				
1943-P	271,165,000				
1943/2-P	Incl. above				
1943-D	15,294,000				
1943-S	104,060,000				
1944-P	119,150,000				
1944-D	32,309,000				
1944-S	21,640,000				
1945-P	119,408,100				
1945-D	37,158,000				
1945-S	58,939,000				
1946	161,116,000				
1946-D	45,292,200				
1946-S	13,560,000				
1947	95,000,000				
1947-D	37,822,000				
1947-S	24,720,000				
1948	89,348,000				
1948-D	44,734,000				
1948-S	11,300,000				
1949	60,652,000				
1949-D	36,498,000				
1949-D/S	Incl. above				
1949-S	9,716,000				
1950	9,796,000				
1950 Proof	51,386				
1950-D	2,630,030				
1951	28,552,000				
1951 Proof	57,500				
1951-D	20,460,000				
1951-S	7,776,000				
1952	63,988,000				
1952 Proof	81,980				
1952-D	30,638,000				

5 cents Jefferson (continued)

	Mintage	Grade	Date purchased	Amount paid	Comments
1952-S	20,572,000				
1953	46,644,000				
1953 Proof	128,800				
1953-D	59,878,600				
1953-S	19,210,900				
1954	47,684,050				
1954 Proof	233,350				
1954-D	117,136,560				
1954-S	29,384,000				
1954 S/D	Incl. above				
1955	7,888,000				
1955 Proof	378,200				
1955-D	74,464,100				
1955 D/S Variety 1	Incl. above				
1956	35,216,000				
1956 Proof	669,384				
1956-D	67,222,640				
1957	38,408,000				
1957 Proof	1,247,952				
1957-D	136,828,900				
1958	17,088,000				
1958 Proof	875,652				
1958-D	168,249,120				
1959	27,248,000				
1959 Proof	1,149,291				
1959-D	160,738,240				
1960	55,416,000				
1960 Proof	1,691,602				
1960-D	192,582,180				
1961	73,640,000				
1961 Proof	3,028,244				
1961-D	229,342,760				
1962	97,384,000				
1962 Proof	3,218,019				
1962-D	280,195,720				
1963	175,776,000				
1963 Proof	3,075,645				
1963-D	276,829,460				
1964	1,024,672,000				

5 cents Jefferson (continued)

	Mintage	Grade	Date purchased	Amount paid	Comments
1964 Proof	3,950,762				
1964-D...............	1,787,297,160				
1965	136,131,380				
1966	156,208,283				
1967	107,325,800				
1968-D...............	91,227,880				
1968-S	100,396,001				
1968-S Proof.	3,041,506				
1969-D...............	202,807,500				
1969-S	120,165,000				
1969-S Proof.	2,934,631				
1970-D...............	515,485,380				
1970-S	238,832,004				
1970-S Proof.	2,632,810				
1971	106,884,000				
1971-D...............	316,144,800				
1971-S Proof.	3,220,733				
1972 .,.................	202,036,000				
1972-D...............	351,694,600				
1972-S Proof.	3,260,996				
1973	384,396,000				
1973-D...............	261,405,400				
1973-S Proof.	2,760,339				
1974	601,752,000				
1974-D...............	277,373,000				
1974-S Proof.	2,612,568				
1975	181,772,000				
1975-D...............	401,875,300				
1975-S Proof.	2,845,450				
1976	367,124,000				
1976-D...............	563,964,147				
1976-S Proof.	4,123,056				
1977	585,376,000				
1977-D...............	297,313,422				
1977-S Proof.	3,236,798				
1978	391,308,000				
1978-D...............	313,092,780				
1978-S Proof.	3,120,285				
1979	463,188,000				

5 cents Jefferson (continued)

	Mintage	Grade	Date purchased	Amount paid	Comments
1979-D	325,867,672				
1979-S Proof.	3,677,175				
1980-P	593,004,000				
1980-D	502,323,448				
1980-S Proof.	3,554,806				
1981-P	657,504,000				
1981-D	364,801,843				
1981-S Proof.	4,063,083				
1982-P	292,355,000				
1982-D	373,726,544				
1982-S Proof.	3,857,479				
1983-P	561,615,000				
1983-D	536,726,276				
1983-S Proof.	3,138,765				
1984-P	746,769,000				
1984-D	517,675,146				
1984-S Proof.	2,748,430				
1985-P	647,114,962				
1985-D	459,747,446				
1985-S Proof.	3,362,821				
1986-P	536,883,493				
1986-D	361,819,144				
1986-S Proof.	2,411,180				
1987-P	371,499,481				
1987-D	410,590,604				
1987-S Proof.	3,715,041				
1988-P	771,360,000				
1988-D	663,771,652				
1988-S Proof.					
1989-P					
1989-D					
1989-S Proof.					
1990-P					
1990-D					
1990-S Proof.					
1991-P					
1991-D					
1991-S Proof.					
1992-P					

5 cents Jefferson (continued)

	Mintage	Grade	Date purchased	Amount paid	Comments
1992-D...............					
1992-S Proof.					
1993-P					
1993-D...............					
1993-S Proof.					
1994-P					
1994-D...............					
1994-S Proof.					
1995-P					
1995-D...............					
1995-S Proof.					

Half dime Flowing Hair

	Mintage	Grade	Date purchased	Amount paid	Comments
1794	7,756				
1795	78,660				

Half dime Draped Bust, Small Eagle or Heraldic Eagle

	Mintage	Grade	Date purchased	Amount paid	Comments
1796 Small Eagle..	10,230				
1796/5	Incl. above				
1796 LIKERTY	Incl. above				
1797 15 Stars	44,527				
1797 16 Stars	Incl. above				
1797 13 Stars	Incl. above				
1800 Heraldic Eagle	24,000				
1800 LIBEKTY	Incl. above				
1801	33,910				
1802	13,010				
1803	37,850				
1805	15,600				

Half dime Capped Bust

	Mintage	Grade	Date purchased	Amount paid	Comments
1829	1,230,000				
1830	1,240,000				
1831	1,242,700				
1832	965,000				
1833	1,370,000				
1834	1,480,000				
1835	2,760,000				
1836	1,900,000				
1837 Small 5c	871,000				
1837 Large 5c	Incl. above				

Half dime Seated Liberty

	Mintage	Grade	Date purchased	Amount paid	Comments
1837	1,405,000				
1837 SD	Incl. above				
1838 Stars, No Drapery	2,255,000				
1838 Small Stars	Incl. above				
1838-O No Stars	115,000				
1839 No Drapery	1,069,150				
1839-O No Drapery	981,550				
1839-O Large O	Incl. above				
1840 No Drapery	1,344,085				
1840 Drapery	Incl. above				

Half dime Seated Liberty (continued)

	Mintage	Grade	Date purchased	Amount paid	Comments
1840-O No Drapery	935,000				
1840-O Drapery...	Incl. above				
1841......................	1,150,000				
1841-O...................	815,000				
1842......................	815,000				
1842-O...................	350,000				
1843......................	1,165,000				
1844......................	430,000				
1844-O...................	220,000				
1845......................	1,564,000				
1846......................	27,000				
1847......................	1,274,000				
1848......................	668,000				
1848 LD.................	Incl. above				
1848-O...................	600,000				
1849/6	1,309,000				
1849/8	Incl. above				
1849......................	Incl. above				
1849-O...................	140,000				
1850......................	955,000				
1850-O...................	690,000				
1851......................	781,000				
1851-O...................	860,000				
1852......................	1,000,500				
1852-O...................	260,000				
1853 No Arrows	135,000				
1853 Arrows	13,210,020				
1853-O No Arrows	160,000				
1853-O Arrows	2,200,000				
1854 Arrows	5,740,000				
1854-O Arrows	1,560,000				
1855 Arrows	1,750,000				
1855-O Arrows	600,000				
1856 No Arrows	4,880,000				
1856-O No Arrows	1,100,000				
1857......................	7,280,000				
1857-O...................	1,380,000				
1858......................	3,500,000				

Half dime Seated Liberty (continued)

	Mintage	Grade	Date purchased	Amount paid	Comments
1858/Inv	Incl. above				
1858/1858	Incl. above				
1858-O	1,660,000				
1859	340,000				
1859-O	560,000				
1860 Legend	798,000				
1860-O	1,060,000				
1861	3,360,000				
1861/O	Incl. above				
1862	1,492,000				
1863	18,000				
1863-S	100,000				
1864	48,000				
1864-S	90,000				
1865	13,000				
1865-S	120,000				
1866	10,000				
1866-S	120,000				
1867	8,000				
1867-S	120,000				
1868	88,600				
1868-S	280,000				
1869	208,000				
1869-S	230,000				
1870	535,600				
1871	1,873,000				
1871-S	161,000				
1872	2,947,000				
1872-S In Wreath	837,000				
1872-S Below Wreath	Incl. above				
1873	712,000				
1873-S	324,000				

Dime Draped Bust, Small Eagle or Heraldic Eagle

	Mintage	Grade	Date purchased	Amount paid	Comments
1796 Small Eagle..	22,135				
1797 16 Stars	25,261				
1797 13 Stars	Incl. above				
1798/97 Heraldic Eagle.	27,550				
1798/97 13 Stars...	Incl. above				
1798....................	Incl. above				
1798 Small 8	Incl. above				
1800....................	21,760				
1801....................	34,640				
1802....................	10,975				
1803....................	33,040				
1804....................	8,265				
1805....................	120,780				
1805 5 Berries........	Incl. above				
1807....................	165,000				

Dime Capped Bust

	Mintage	Grade	Date purchased	Amount paid	Comments
1809....................	51,065				
1811/9	65,180				

Dime Capped Bust (continued)

	Mintage	Grade	Date purchased	Amount paid	Comments
1814 Small Date...	421,500				
1814 Large Date..	Incl. above				
1814 S of A	Incl. above				
1820 Large O	942,587				
1820 Small O	Incl. above				
1820 S of A	Incl. above				
1821 Small Date ...	1,186,512				
1821 Large Date..	Incl. above				
1822	100,000				
1823/2....................	440,000				
1824/2....................	100,000				
1825	410,000				
1827	1,215,000				
1828 Large Date..	125,000				
1828 Small Date ...	Incl. above				
1829 Curl Base 2..	770,000				
1829 Small 10c......	Incl. above				
1829 Large 10c	Incl. above				
1830	510,000				
1830/29.................	Incl. above				
1831	771,350				
1832	522,500				
1833	485,000				
1834	635,000				
1835	1,410,000				
1836	1,190,000				
1837	359,500				

Dime Seated Liberty

	Mintage	Grade	Date purchased	Amount paid	Comments
1837 No Stars........	682,500				
1838 Small Stars ...	1,992,500				
1838 Large Stars ...	Incl. above				
1838-O..................	406,034				
1839.....................	1,053,115				
1839-O..................	1,323,000				
1840 No Drapery..	1,358,580				
1840 Drapery........	Incl. above				
1840-O No Drapery	1,175,000				
1841......................	1,622,500				
1841-O..................	2,007,500				
1842......................	1,887,500				
1842-O..................	2,020,000				
1843......................	1,370,000				
1843-O..................	50,000				
1844......................	72,500				
1845......................	1,755,000				
1845-O..................	230,000				
1846......................	31,300				
1847......................	245,000				
1848......................	451,500				
1849......................	839,000				
1849-O..................	300,000				
1850......................	1,931,500				
1850-O..................	510,000				
1851......................	1,026,500				
1851-O..................	400,000				
1852......................	1,535,500				
1852-O..................	430,000				
1853 No Arrows	95,000				

Dime Seated Liberty (continued)

	Mintage	Grade	Date purchased	Amount paid	Comments
1853 Arrows	12,078,010				
1853-O Arrows	1,100,000				
1854 Arrows	4,470,000				
1854-O Arrows	1,770,000				
1855 Arrows	2,075,000				
1856 SD No Arrows	5,780,000				
1856 Large Date	Incl. above				
1856-O	1,180,000				
1856-S	70,000				
1857	5,580,000				
1857-O	1,540,000				
1858	1,540,000				
1858-O	290,000				
1858-S	60,000				
1859	430,000				
1859-O	480,000				
1859-S	60,000				
1860 Legend	606,000				
1860-O	40,000				
1860-S	140,000				
1861	1,883,000				
1861-S	172,500				
1862	847,000				
1862-S	180,750				
1863	14,000				
1863-S	157,500				
1864	11,000				
1864-S	230,000				
1865	10,000				
1865-S	175,000				
1866	8,000				
1866-S	135,000				
1867	6,000				
1867-S	140,000				
1868	464,000				
1868-S	260,000				
1869	256,000				
1869-S	450,000				

Dime Seated Liberty (continued)

	Mintage	Grade	Date purchased	Amount paid	Comments
1870	470,500				
1870-S	50,000				
1871	906,750				
1871-CC	20,100				
1871-S	320,000				
1872	2,395,500				
1872-CC	35,480				
1872-S	190,000				
1873 Closed 3	1,568,000				
1873 Open 3	Incl. above				
1873 Arrows	2,377,700				
1873-CC Arrows	18,791				
1873-S	455,000				
1874	2,940,000				
1874-CC	10,817				
1874-S	240,000				
1875 No Arrows	10,350,000				
1875-CC Below Wreath	4,645,000				
1875-CC In Wreath	Incl. above				
1875-S Below Wreath	9,070,000				
1876	11,460,000				
1876-CC	8,270,000				
1876-S	10,420,000				
1877	7,310,000				
1877-CC	7,700,000				
1877-S	2,340,000				
1878	1,678,000				
1878-CC	200,000				
1879	14,000				
1880	36,000				
1881	24,000				
1882	3,910,000				
1883	7,674,673				
1884	3,365,505				
1884-S	564,969				
1885	2,532,497				
1885-S	43,690				

Dime Seated Liberty (continued)

	Mintage	Grade	Date purchased	Amount paid	Comments
1886	6,376,684				
1886-S	206,524				
1887	11,283,229				
1887-S	4,454,450				
1888	5,495,655				
1888-S	1,720,000				
1889	7,380,000				
1889-S	972,678				
1890	9,910,951				
1890-S	1,423,076				
1891	15,310,000				
1891-O	4,540,000				
1891-S	3,196,116				

Dime Barber

	Mintage	Grade	Date purchased	Amount paid	Comments
1892	12,120,000				
1892-O	3,841,700				
1892-S	990,710				
1893	3,340,000				
1893/2	Incl. above				
1893-O	1,760,000				
1893-S	2,491,401				
1894	1,330,000				
1894-O	720,000				
1894-S	24				
1895	690,000				
1895-O	440,000				
1895-S	1,120,000				
1896	2,000,000				

Dime Barber (continued)

	Mintage	Grade	Date purchased	Amount paid	Comments
1896-O	610,000				
1896-S	575,056				
1897	10,868,533				
1897-O	666,000				
1897-S	1,342,844				
1898	16,320,000				
1898-O	2,130,000				
1898-S	1,702,507				
1899	19,580,000				
1899-O	2,650,000				
1899-S	1,867,493				
1900	17,600,000				
1900-O	2,010,000				
1900-S	5,168,270				
1901	18,859,665				
1901-O	5,620,000				
1901-S	593,022				
1902	21,380,000				
1902-O	4,500,000				
1902-S	2,070,000				
1903	19,500,000				
1903-O	8,180,000				
1903-S	613,300				
1904	14,600,357				
1904-S	800,000				
1905	14,551,623				
1905-O	3,400,000				
1905-S	6,855,199				
1906	19,957,731				
1906-D	4,060,000				
1906-O	2,610,000				
1906-S	3,136,640				
1907	22,220,000				
1907-D	4,080,000				
1907-O	5,058,000				
1907-S	3,178,470				
1908	10,600,000				
1908-D	7,490,000				
1908-O	1,789,000				

Dime Barber (continued)

	Mintage	Grade	Date purchased	Amount paid	Comments
1908-S	3,220,000				
1909	10,240,000				
1909-D	954,000				
1909-O	2,287,000				
1909-S	1,000,000				
1910	11,520,000				
1910-D	3,490,000				
1910-S	1,240,000				
1911	18,870,000				
1911-D	11,209,000				
1911-S	3,520,000				
1912	19,350,000				
1912-D	11,760,000				
1912-S	3,420,000				
1913	19,760,000				
1913-S	510,000				
1914	17,360,230				
1914-D	11,908,000				
1914-S	2,100,000				
1915	5,620,000				
1915-S	960,000				
1916	18,490,000				
1916-S	5,820,000				

Dime Winged Liberty Head ("Mercury")

	Mintage	Grade	Date purchased	Amount paid	Comments
1916	22,180,080				
1916-D	264,000				
1916-S	10,450,000				

Dime Winged Liberty Head (continued)

	Mintage	Grade	Date purchased	Amount paid	Comments
1917	55,230,000				
1917-D	9,402,000				
1917-S	27,330,000				
1918	26,680,000				
1918-D	22,674,800				
1918-S	19,300,000				
1919	35,740,000				
1919-D	9,939,000				
1919-S	8,850,000				
1920	59,030,000				
1920-D	19,171,000				
1920-S	13,820,000				
1921	1,230,000				
1921-D	1,080,000				
1923	50,130,000				
1923-S	6,440,000				
1924	24,010,000				
1924-D	6,810,000				
1924-S	7,120,000				
1925	25,610,000				
1925-D	5,117,000				
1925-S	5,850,000				
1926	32,160,000				
1926-D	6,828,000				
1926-S	1,520,000				
1927	28,080,000				
1927-D	4,812,000				
1927-S	4,770,000				
1928	19,480,000				
1928-D	4,161,000				
1928-S	7,400,000				
1929	25,970,000				
1929-D	5,034,000				
1929-S	4,730,000				
1930	6,770,000				
1930-S	1,843,000				
1931	3,150,000				
1931-D	1,260,000				
1931-S	1,800,000				

Dime Winged Liberty Head (continued)

	Mintage	Grade	Date purchased	Amount paid	Comments
1934	24,080,000				
1934-D	6,772,000				
1935	58,830,000				
1935-D	10,477,000				
1935-S	15,840,000				
1936	87,500,000				
1936-D	16,132,000				
1936-S	9,210,000				
1936 Proof.	4,130				
1937	56,860,000				
1937-D	14,146,000				
1937-S	9,740,000				
1937 Proof.	5,756				
1938	22,190,000				
1938-D	5,537,000				
1938-S	8,090,000				
1938 Proof.	8,728				
1939	67,740,000				
1939-D	24,394,000				
1939-S	10,540,000				
1939 Proof.	9,321				
1940	65,350,000				
1940-D	21,198,000				
1940-S	21,560,000				
1940 Proof.	11,827				
1941	175,090,000				
1941-D	45,634,000				
1941-S	43,090,000				
1941 Proof.	16,557				
1942/1	205,410,000				
1942/1-D	Incl. above				
1942	Incl. above				
1942-D	60,740,000				
1942-S	49,300,000				
1942 Proof.	22,329				
1943	191,710,000				
1943-D	71,949,000				
1943-S	60,400,000				
1944	231,410,000				

Dime Winged Liberty Head (continued)

	Mintage	Grade	Date purchased	Amount paid	Comments
1944-D	62,224,000				
1944-S	49,490,000				
1945	159,130,000				
1945-D	40,245,000				
1945-S	41,920,000				
1945 Micro S	Incl. above				

Dime Roosevelt

	Mintage	Grade	Date purchased	Amount paid	Comments
1946	255,250,000				
1946-D	61,043,500				
1946-S	27,900,000				
1947	121,520,000				
1947-D	46,835,000				
1947-S	34,840,000				
1948	74,950,000				
1948-D	52,841,000				
1948-S	35,520,000				
1949	30,940,000				
1949-D	26,034,000				
1949-S	13,510,000				
1950	50,130,114				
1950 Proof	51,386				
1950-D	46,803,000				
1950-S	20,440,000				
1951	102,880,102				
1951 Proof	57,500				
1951-D	56,529,000				
1951-S	31,630,000				
1952	99,040,093				

Dime Roosevelt (continued)

	Mintage	Grade	Date purchased	Amount paid	Comments
1952 Proof	81,980				
1952-D..................	122,100,000				
1952-S	44,419,500				
1953	53,490,120				
1953 Proof	128,800				
1953-D..................	136,433,000				
1953-S	39,180,000				
1954	114,010,203				
1954 Proof	233,350				
1954-D..................	106,397,000				
1954-S	22,860,000				
1955	12,450,181				
1955 Proof	378,200				
1955-D..................	13,959,000				
1955-S	18,510,000				
1956	108,640,000				
1956 Proof	669,384				
1956-D..................	108,015,100				
1957	160,160,000				
1957 Proof	1,247,952				
1957-D..................	113,354,330				
1958	31,910,000				
1958 Proof	875,652				
1958-D..................	136,564,600				
1959	85,780,000				
1959 Proof	1,149,291				
1959-D..................	164,919,790				
1960	70,390,000				
1960 Proof	1,691,602				
1960-D..................	200,160,400				
1961	93,730,000				
1961 Proof	3,028,244				
1961-D..................	209,146,550				
1962	72,450,000				
1962 Proof	3,218,019				
1962-D..................	334,948,380				
1963	123,650,000				
1963 Proof	3,075,645				
1963-D..................	421,476,530				

Dime Roosevelt (continued)

	Mintage	Grade	Date purchased	Amount paid	Comments
1964	929,360,000				
1964 Proof	3,950,762				
1964-D	1,357,517,180				
1965	1,652,140,470				
1966	1,382,734,540				
1967	2,224,007,320				
1968	424,470,000				
1968-D	480,748,280				
1968-S Proof	3,041,506				
1969	145,790,000				
1969-D	563,323,870				
1969-S Proof	2,934,631				
1970	345,570,000				
1970-D	754,042,100				
1970-S Proof	2,632,810				
1971	162,690,000				
1971-D	377,914,240				
1971-S Proof	3,220,733				
1972	431,540,000				
1972-D	330,290,000				
1972-S Proof	3,260,996				
1973	315,670,000				
1973-D	455,032,426				
1973-S Proof	2,760,339				
1974	470,248,000				
1974-D	571,083,000				
1974-S Proof	2,612,568				
1975	585,673,900				
1975-D	313,705,300				
1975-S Proof	2,845,450				
1976	568,760,000				
1976-D	695,222,774				
1976-S Proof	4,123,056				
1977	796,930,000				
1977-D	376,607,228				
1977-S Proof	3,236,798				
1978	663,980,000				
1978-D	282,847,540				
1978-S Proof	3,120,285				

Dime Roosevelt (continued)

	Mintage	Grade	Date purchased	Amount paid	Comments
1979	315,440,000				
1979-D..................	390,921,184				
1979-S Proof.	3,677,175				
1980-P..................	735,170,000				
1980-D..................	719,354,321				
1980-S Proof.	3,554,806				
1981-P..................	676,650,000				
1981-D..................	712,284,143				
1981-S Proof.	4,063,083				
1982-P.	519,475,000				
1982 No Mint Mark, Strong Strike..................	Incl. above				
1982-D.	542,713,584				
1982-S Proof.	3,857,479				
1983-P..................	647,025,000				
1983-D.	730,129,224				
1983-S Proof.	3,138,765				
1984-P..................	856,669,000				
1984-D.	704,803,976				
1984-S Proof.	2,748,430				
1985-P..................	705,200,962				
1985-D.	587,979,970				
1985-S Proof.	3,362,821				
1986-P..................	682,649,693				
1986-D.	473,326,974				
1986-S Proof.	2,411,180				
1987-P..................	762,709,481				
1987-D.	653,203,402				
1987-S Proof.	3,715,041				
1988-P..................	1,030,550,000				
1988-D.	962,385,488				
1988-S. Proof					
1989-P..................					
1989-D.					
1989-S..................					
1990-P.					
1990-D.					
1990-S..................					

Dime Roosevelt (continued)

	Mintage	Grade	Date purchased	Amount paid	Comments
1991-P.					
1991-D.					
1991-S.					
1992-P.					
1992-D.					
1992-S.					
1993-P.					
1993-D.					
1993-S.					
1994-P.					
1994-D.					
1994-S.					
1995-P.					
1995-D.					
1995-S.					

20 cents

	Mintage	Grade	Date purchased	Amount paid	Comments
1875	38,500				
1875-CC.	133,290				
1875-S.	1,155,000				
1876	14,750				
1876-CC	10,000				
1877 Proof	510				
1878 Proof	600				

Quarter dollar Draped Bust, Small Eagle or Heraldic Eagle

	Mintage	Grade	Date purchased	Amount paid	Comments
1796 Small Eagle ..	6,146				
1804 Heraldic Eagle	6,738				
1805	121,394				
1806/5	286,424				
1806	Incl. above				
1807	140,343				

Quarter dollar Capped Bust

	Mintage	Grade	Date purchased	Amount paid	Comments
1815	89,235				
1818/5	361,174				
1818	Incl. above				
1819	144,000				
1820 Small O	127,444				
1820 Large O	Incl. above				

Quarter dollar Capped Bust (continued)

	Mintage	Grade	Date purchased	Amount paid	Comments
1821	216,851				
1822	64,080				
1822 25/50c	Incl. above				
1823/22	17,800				
1824/2	24,000				
1825/2	148,000				
1825	Incl. above				
1825/4	Incl. above				
1827	(R)				
1828	102,000				
1828 25/50c	Incl. above				
1831 No Motto	398,000				
1832	320,000				
1833	156,000				
1834	286,000				
1835	1,952,000				
1836	472,000				
1837	252,400				

Quarter dollar Seated Liberty

	Mintage	Grade	Date purchased	Amount paid	Comments
1838	366,000				
1838 No Drapery	466,000				
1839 No Drapery	491,146				
1840 Drapery	188,127				
1840-O No Drapery	382,200				
1840-O Drapery	43,000				

Quarter dollar Seated Liberty (continued)

	Mintage	Grade	Date purchased	Amount paid	Comments
1841	120,000				
1841-O	452,000				
1842 Large Date.	88,000				
1842-O Small Date	769,000				
1842-O Large Date	Incl. above				
1843	645,600				
1843-O	968,000				
1844	421,200				
1844-O	740,000				
1845	922,000				
1846	510,000				
1847	734,000				
1847-O	368,000				
1848	146,000				
1849	340,000				
1849-O	16,000				
1850	190,800				
1850-O	396,000				
1851	160,000				
1851-O	88,000				
1852	177,060				
1852-O	96,000				
1853/53 Recut Date	44,200				
1853 Arrows & Rays	15,210,020				
1853/4 Arrows & Rays	Incl. above				
1853-O Arrows & Rays	1,332,000				
1854 Arrows	12,380,000				
1854-O Arrows.	1,484,000				
1854-O Huge O	Incl. above				
1855 Arrows	2,857,000				
1855-O Arrows	176,000				
1855-S Arrows	396,400				
1856 No Arrows	7,264,000				
1856-O	968,000				
1856-S	286,000				
1856-S/S	Incl. above				

Quarter dollar Seated Liberty (continued)

	Mintage	Grade	Date purchased	Amount paid	Comments
1857	9,644,000				
1857-O	1,180,000				
1857-S	82,000				
1858	7,368,000				
1858-O	520,000				
1858-S	121,000				
1859	1,344,000				
1859-O	260,000				
1859-S	80,000				
1860	804,400				
1860-O	388,000				
1860-S	56,000				
1861	4,853,600				
1861-S	96,000				
1862	932,000				
1862-S	67,000				
1863	191,600				
1864	93,600				
1864-S	20,000				
1865	58,800				
1865-S	41,000				
1866 Motto	16,800				
1866-S	28,000				
1867	20,000				
1867-S	48,000				
1868	29,400				
1868-S	96,000				
1869	16,000				
1869-S	76,000				
1870	86,400				
1870-CC	8,340				
1871	117,200				
1871-CC	10,890				
1871-S	30,900				
1872	182,000				
1872-CC	22,850				
1872-S	83,000				
1873 Closed 3	212,000				
1873 Open 3	Incl. above				

Quarter dollar Seated Liberty (continued)

	Mintage	Grade	Date purchased	Amount paid	Comments
1873 Arrows	1,271,160				
1873-CC Arrows	12,462				
1873-S Arrows	156,000				
1874 Arrows	471,200				
1874-S Arrows	392,000				
1875	4,292,800				
1875-CC	140,000				
1875-S	680,000				
1876	17,816,000				
1876-CC	4,944,000				
1876-S	8,596,000				
1877	10,911,200				
1877-CC	4,192,000				
1877-S	8,996,000				
1877-S/Horizontal S	Incl. above				
1878	2,260,000				
1878-CC	996,000				
1878-S	140,000				
1879	14,450				
1880	13,600				
1881	12,000				
1882	15,200				
1883	14,400				
1884	8,000				
1885	13,600				
1886	5,000				
1887	10,000				
1888	10,001				
1888-S	1,216,000				
1889	12,000				
1890	80,000				
1891	3,920,000				
1891-O	68,000				
1891-S	2,216,000				

Quarter dollar Barber

	Mintage	Grade	Date purchased	Amount paid	Comments
1892	8,236,000				
1892-O	2,640,000				
1892-S	964,079				
1893	5,444,023				
1893-O	3,396,000				
1893-S	1,454,535				
1894	3,432,000				
1894-O	2,852,000				
1894-S	2,648,821				
1895	4,440,000				
1895-O	2,816,000				
1895-S	1,764,611				
1896	3,874,000				
1896-O	1,484,000				
1896-S	188,039				
1897	8,140,000				
1897-O	1,414,800				
1897-S	542,229				
1898	11,100,000				
1898-O	1,868,000				
1898-S	1,020,592				
1899	12,624,000				
1899-O	2,644,000				
1899-S	708,000				
1900	10,016,000				
1900-O	3,416,000				
1900-S	1,858,585				
1901	8,892,000				

Quarter dollar Barber (continued)

	Mintage	Grade	Date purchased	Amount paid	Comments
1901-O	1,612,000				
1901-S	72,664				
1902	12,196,967				
1902-O	4,748,000				
1902-S	1,524,612				
1903	9,669,309				
1903-O	3,500,000				
1903-S	1,036,000				
1904	9,588,143				
1904-O	2,456,000				
1905	4,967,523				
1905-O	1,230,000				
1905-S	1,884,000				
1906	3,655,760				
1906-D	3,280,000				
1906-O	2,056,000				
1907	7,192,000				
1907-D	2,484,000				
1907-O	4,560,000				
1907-S	1,360,000				
1908	4,232,000				
1908-D	5,788,000				
1908-O	6,244,000				
1908-S	784,000				
1909	9,268,000				
1909-D	5,114,000				
1909-O	712,000				
1909-S	1,348,000				
1910	2,244,000				
1910-D	1,500,000				
1911	3,720,000				
1911-D	933,600				
1911-S	988,000				
1912	4,400,000				
1912-S	708,000				
1913	484,000				
1913-D	1,450,800				
1913-S	40,000				
1914	6,244,230				

Quarter dollar Barber (continued)

	Mintage	Grade	Date purchased	Amount paid	Comments
1914-D	3,046,000				
1914-S	264,000				
1915	3,480,000				
1915-D	3,694,000				
1915-S	704,000				
1916	1,788,000				
1916-D	6,540,800				

Quarter dollar Standing Liberty

	Mintage	Grade	Date purchased	Amount paid	Comments
1916	52,000				
1917 Bare Breast	8,740,000				
1917-D Bare Breast	1,509,200				
1917-S Bare Breast	1,952,000				
1917 Mailed Breast	13,880,000				
1917-D Mailed Breast	6,224,400				
1917-S Mailed Breast	5,552,000				
1918	14,240,000				
1918-D	7,380,000				
1918-S	11,072,000				
1918/7-S	Incl. above				
1919	11,324,000				
1919-D	1,944,000				
1919-S	1,836,000				
1920	27,860,000				

Quarter dollar Standing Liberty (continued)

	Mintage	Grade	Date purchased	Amount paid	Comments
1920-D..............	3,586,400				
1920-S	6,380,000				
1921	1,916,000				
1923	9,716,000				
1923-S	1,360,000				
1924	10,920,000				
1924-D..............	3,112,000				
1924-S	2,860,000				
1925	12,280,000				
1926	11,316,000				
1926-D..............	1,716,000				
1926-S	2,700,000				
1927	11,912,000				
1927-D..............	976,400				
1927-S	396,000				
1928	6,336,000				
1928-D..............	1,627,600				
1928-S	2,644,000				
1929	11,140,000				
1929-D..............	1,358,000				
1929-S	1,764,000				
1930	5,632,000				
1930-S	1,556,000				

Quarter dollar Washington

	Mintage	Grade	Date purchased	Amount paid	Comments
1932	5,404,000				

Quarter dollar Washington (continued)

	Mintage	Grade	Date purchased	Amount paid	Comments
1932-D	436,800				
1932-S	408,000				
1934 Heavy Motto	31,912,052				
1934 Light Motto	Incl. above				
1934 Doubled Die	Incl. above				
1934-D	3,527,200				
1935	32,484,000				
1935-D	5,780,000				
1935-S	5,660,000				
1936	41,300,000				
1936-D	5,374,000				
1936-S	3,828,000				
1936 Proof	3,837				
1937	19,696,000				
1937-D	7,189,600				
1937-S	1,652,000				
1937 Proof	5,542				
1938	9,472,000				
1938-S	2,832,000				
1938 Proof	8,045				
1939	33,540,000				
1939-D	7,092,000				
1939-S	2,628,000				
1939 Proof	8,795				
1940	35,704,000				
1940-D	2,797,600				
1940-S	8,244,000				
1940 Proof	11,246				
1941	79,032,000				
1941-D	16,714,800				
1941-S	16,080,000				
1941 Proof	15,287				
1942	102,096,000				
1942-D	17,487,200				
1942-S	19,384,000				
1942 Proof	21,123				
1943	99,700,000				
1943-D	16,095,600				

Quarter dollar Washington (continued)

	Mintage	Grade	Date purchased	Amount paid	Comments
1943-S	21,700,000				
1943-S Doubled Die......................	Incl. above				
1944	104,956,000				
1944-D....................	14,600,800				
1944-S	12,560,000				
1945	74,372,000				
1945-D....................	12,341,600				
1945-S	17,004,001				
1946	53,436,000				
1946-D....................	9,072,800				
1946-S	4,204,000				
1947	22,556,000				
1947-D....................	15,338,400				
1947-S	5,532,000				
1948	35,196,000				
1948-D....................	16,766,800				
1948-S	15,960,000				
1949	9,312,000				
1949-D....................	10,068,400				
1950	24,920,126				
1950 Proof	51,386				
1950-D....................	21,075,600				
1950-D/S..............	Incl. above				
1950-S	10,284,004				
1950-S/D..............	Incl. above				
1951	43,448,102				
1951 Proof	57,500				
1951-D....................	35,354,800				
1951-S	9,048,000				
1952	38,780,093				
1952 Proof	81,980				
1952-D....................	49,795,200				
1952-S	13,707,800				
1953	18,536,120				
1953 Proof	128,800				
1953-D....................	56,112,400				
1953-S	14,016,000				
1954	54,412,203				

Quarter dollar Washington (continued)

	Mintage	Grade	Date purchased	Amount paid	Comments
1954 Proof	233,350				
1954-D	42,305,500				
1954-S	11,834,722				
1955	18,180,181				
1955 Proof	378,200				
1955-D	3,182,400				
1956	44,144,000				
1956 Proof	669,384				
1956-D	32,334,500				
1957	46,532,000				
1957 Proof	1,247,952				
1957-D	77,924,160				
1958	6,360,000				
1958 Proof	875,652				
1958-D	78,124,900				
1959	24,384,000				
1959 Proof	1,149,291				
1959-D	62,054,232				
1960	29,164,000				
1960 Proof	1,691,602				
1960-D	63,000,324				
1961	37,036,000				
1961 Proof	3,028,244				
1961-D	83,656,928				
1962	36,156,000				
1962 Proof	3,218,019				
1962-D	127,554,756				
1963	74,316,000				
1963 Proof	3,075,645				
1963-D	135,288,184				
1964	560,390,585				
1964 Proof	3,950,762				
1964-D	704,135,528				
1965	1,819,717,540				
1966	821,101,500				
1967	1,524,031,848				
1968	220,731,500				
1968-D	101,534,000				
1968-S Proof.	3,041,506				

Quarter dollar Washington (continued)

	Mintage	Grade	Date purchased	Amount paid	Comments
1969	176,212,000				
1969-D..................	114,372,000				
1969-S Proof.	2,934,631				
1970	136,420,000				
1970-D..................	417,341,364				
1970-S Proof.	2,632,810				
1971	109,284,000				
1971-D..................	258,634,428				
1971-S Proof.	3,220,733				
1972	215,048,000				
1972-D..................	311,067,732				
1972-S Proof.	3,260,996				
1973	346,924,000				
1973-D..................	232,977,400				
1973-S Proof.	2,760,339				
1974	801,456,000				
1974-D..................	353,160,300				
1974-S Proof.	2,612,568				
1776-1976	809,784,016				
1776-1976-D..........	860,118,839				
1776-1976-S	6,968,506				
1776-1976-S 40% silver					
Proof....................	3,998,621				
Uncirculated......	4,908,319				
1977	468,556,000				
1977-D..................	256,524,978				
1977-S Proof.	3,236,798				
1978	521,452,000				
1978-D..................	287,373,152				
1978-S Proof.	3,120,285				
1979	515,708,000				
1979-D..................	489,789,780				
1979-S Proof.	3,677,175				
1980 -P.	635,832,000				
1980-D..................	518,327,487				
1980-S Proof.	3,554,806				
1981-P	601,716,000				
1981-D..................	575,722,833				
1981-S Proof.	4,063,083				

Quarter dollar Washington (continued)

	Mintage	Grade	Date purchased	Amount paid	Comments
1982-P.	500,931,000				
1982-D.	480,042,788				
1982-S Proof.	3,857,479				
1983-P.	673,535,000				
1983-D.	617,806,446				
1983-S Proof.	3,138,765				
1984-P.	676,545,000				
1984-D.	546,483,064				
1984-S Proof.	2,748,430				
1985-P.	775,818,962				
1985-D.	519,962,888				
1985-S Proof.	3,362,821				
1986-P.	551,199,333				
1986-D.	504,298,660				
1986-S Proof.	2,411,180				
1987-P.	582,499,481				
1987-D.	655,594,696				
1987-S Proof.	3,715,041				
1988-P.	562,052,000				
1988-D.	596,810,688				
1988-S Proof.					
1989-P.					
1989-D.					
1989-S Proof.					
1990-P.					
1990-D.					
1990-S Proof.					
1991-P.					
1991-D.					
1991-S Proof.					
1992-P.					
1992-D.					
1992-S Proof.					
1993-P.					
1993-D.					
1993-S Proof.					
1994-P.					
1994-D.					
1994-S Proof.					

Quarter dollar Washington (continued)

	Mintage	Grade	Date purchased	Amount paid	Comments
1995-P....................					
1995-D.					
1995-S Proof.					

Half dollar Flowing Hair

	Mintage	Grade	Date purchased	Amount paid	Comments
1794	23,464				
1795	299,680				
1795 3 Leaves.......	Incl. above				

Half dollar Draped Bust, Small Eagle

	Mintage	Grade	Date purchased	Amount paid	Comments
1796 15 Stars	934				
1796 16 Stars	Incl. above				
1797 15 Stars	2,984				

Half dollar Draped Bust, Heraldic Eagle

	Mintage	Grade	Date purchased	Amount paid	Comments
1801	30,289				
1802	29,890				
1803 Small 3	188,234				
1803 Large 3	Incl. above				
1805/4	211,722				
1805	Incl. above				

Half dollar Draped Bust, Heraldic Eagle (continued)

	Mintage	Grade	Date purchased	Amount paid	Comments
1806/5	839,576				
1806 6/Inverted 6	Incl. above				
1806	Incl. above				
1807	301,076				

Half dollar Capped Bust

	Mintage	Grade	Date purchased	Amount paid	Comments
1807 Small Stars	750,500				
1807 Large Stars	Incl. above				
1807 50/20	Incl. above				
1808/7	1,368,600				
1808	Incl. above				
1809	1,405,810				
1810	1,276,276				
1811 Small 8	1,203,644				
1811 Large 8	Incl. above				
1811/10	Incl. above				
1812/1	1,628,059				
1812	Incl. above				
1813	1,241,903				
1813 50C/UNI	Incl. above				
1814	1,039,075				
1814/3	Incl. above				
1815/2	47,150				
1817/3	1,215,567				

Half dollar Capped Bust (continued)

	Mintage	Grade	Date purchased	Amount paid	Comments
1817/4	Incl. above				
1817	Incl. above				
1818/7	1,960,322				
1818	Incl. above				
1819/8	2,208,000				
1819	Incl. above				
1820/19	751,122				
1820	Incl. above				
1821	1,305,797				
1822	1,559,573				
1822/1	Incl. above				
1823	1,694,200				
1823 Broken 3	Incl. above				
1824/1	3,504,954				
1824/4	Incl. above				
1824	Incl. above				
1825	2,943,166				
1826	4,004,180				
1827/6	5,493,400				
1827 Square 2	Incl. above				
1827 Curl 2	Incl. above				
1828	3,075,200				
1828 Large 8s	Incl. above				
1828 Small 8s	Incl. above				
1829/7	3,712,156				
1829	Incl. above				
1830 Large O	4,764,800				
1830 Small O	Incl. above				
1831	5,873,660				
1832 Normal	4,797,000				
1832 Large Letters	Incl. above				
1833	5,206,000				
1834	6,412,004				
1835	5,352,006				
1836	6,545,000				
1836 5O/OO	Incl. above				
1836 50 CENTS, Reeded Edge	1,200				
1837 50 CENTS	3,629,820				

Half dollar Capped Bust (continued)

	Mintage	Grade	Date purchased	Amount paid	Comments
1838	3,546,000				
1838	1,362,160				
1839-O..................	178,967				

Half dollar Seated Liberty

	Mintage	Grade	Date purchased	Amount paid	Comments
1839 No Drapery ..	1,972,400				
1839 Drapery	Incl. above				
1840 Sm. Letters...	1,435,008				
1840 Med. Letters	Incl. above				
1840-O..................	855,100				
1841	310,000				
1841-O..................	401,000				
1842 Small Date ...	2,012,764				
1842 Medium Date..................	Incl. above				
1842-O Small Date.	957,000				
1842 Medium Date..................	Incl. above				
1842-O Large Date..................	Incl. above				
1843	3,844,000				
1843-O..................	2,268,000				
1844	1,766,000				
1844-O..................	2,005,000				
1844-O Doubled Date..................	Incl. above				
1845	589,000				

Half dollar Seated Liberty (continued)

	Mintage	Grade	Date purchased	Amount paid	Comments
1845-O....................	2,094,000				
1845-O No Drapery	Incl. above				
1846 Small Date ...	2,210,000				
1846 Tall Date	Incl. above				
1846/Horizontal 6	Incl. above				
1846-O Medium Date...................	2,304,000				
1846-O Tall Date ...	Incl. above				
1847.......................	1,156,000				
1847-O....................	2,584,000				
1847/6	Incl. above				
1848.......................	580,000				
1848-O....................	3,180,000				
1849.......................	1,252,000				
1849-O....................	2,310,000				
1850.......................	227,000				
1850-O....................	2,456,000				
1851.......................	200,750				
1851-O....................	402,000				
1852.......................	77,130				
1852-O....................	144,000				
1853 Arrows & Rays	3,532,708				
1853-O Arrows & Rays	1,328,000				
1854 Arrows	2,982,000				
1854-O Arrows	5,240,000				
1855/1854	759,500				
1855 Arrows	Incl. above				
1855-O Arrows	3,688,000				
1855-S Arrows	129,950				
1856 No Arrows	938,000				
1856-O....................	2,658,000				
1856-S....................	211,000				
1857.......................	1,988,000				
1857-O....................	818,000				
1857-S....................	158,000				
1858.......................	4,226,000				
1858-O....................	7,294,000				
1858-S....................	476,000				

Half dollar Seated Liberty (continued)

	Mintage	Grade	Date purchased	Amount paid	Comments
1859	748,000				
1859-O	2,834,000				
1859-S	566,000				
1860	302,700				
1860-O	1,290,000				
1860-S	472,000				
1861	2,887,400				
1861-O	2,532,633				
1861-S	939,500				
1862	253,000				
1862-S	1,352,000				
1863	503,200				
1863-S	916,000				
1864	379,100				
1864-S	658,000				
1865	511,400				
1865-S	675,000				
1866 Motto	744,900				
1866-S	1,054,000				
1866-S Motto	Incl. above				
1867	449,300				
1867-S	1,196,000				
1868	417,600				
1868-S	1,160,000				
1869	795,300				
1869-S	656,000				
1870	633,900				
1870-CC	54,617				
1870-S	1,004,000				
1871	1,203,600				
1871-CC	153,950				
1871-S	2,178,000				
1872	880,600				
1872-CC	257,000				
1872-S	580,000				
1873 Closed 3	801,200				
1873 Open 3 No Arrows	Incl. above				
1873 Arrows	1,815,150				

Half dollar Seated Liberty (continued)

	Mintage	Grade	Date purchased	Amount paid	Comments
1873-CC	122,500				
1873-CC Arrows...	214,560				
1873-S Arrows	228,000				
1874 Arrows	2,359,600				
1874-CC Arrows...	59,000				
1874-S Arrows	394,000				
1875	6,026,800				
1875-CC	1,008,000				
1875-S	3,200,000				
1876	8,418,000				

Half dollar Barber

	Mintage	Grade	Date purchased	Amount paid	Comments
1892	934,245				
1892-O	390,000				
1892-S	1,029,028				
1893	1,826,000				
1893-O	1,389,000				
1893-S	740,000				
1894	1,148,000				
1894-O	2,138,000				
1894-S	4,048,690				
1895	1,834,338				
1895-O	1,766,000				
1895-S	1,108,086				
1896	950,000				
1896-O	924,000				
1896-S	1,140,948				
1897	2,480,000				
1897-O	632,000				
1897-S	933,900				
1898	2,956,000				
1898-O	874,000				
1898-S	2,358,550				
1899	5,538,000				
1899-O	1,724,000				
1899-S	1,686,411				
1900	4,762,000				
1900-O	2,744,000				
1900-S	2,560,322				
1901	4,268,000				

Half dollar Barber (continued)

	Mintage	Grade	Date purchased	Amount paid	Comments
1901-O	1,124,000				
1901-S	847,044				
1902	4,922,000				
1902-O	2,526,000				
1902-S	1,460,670				
1903	2,278,000				
1903-O	2,100,000				
1903-S	1,920,772				
1904	2,992,000				
1904-O	1,117,600				
1904-S	553,038				
1905	662,000				
1905-O	505,000				
1905-S	2,494,000				
1906	2,638,000				
1906-D	4,028,000				
1906-O	2,446,000				
1906-S	1,740,154				
1907	2,598,000				
1907-D	3,856,000				
1907-O	3,946,600				
1907-S	1,250,000				
1908	1,354,000				
1908-D	3,280,000				
1908-O	5,360,000				
1908-S	1,644,828				
1909	2,368,000				
1909-O	925,400				
1909-S	1,764,000				
1910	418,000				
1910-S	1,948,000				
1911	1,406,000				
1911-D	695,080				
1911-S	1,272,000				
1912	1,550,000				
1912-D	2,300,800				
1912-S	1,370,000				
1913	188,000				
1913-D	534,000				

Half dollar Barber (continued)

	Mintage	Grade	Date purchased	Amount paid	Comments
1913-S	604,000				
1914	124,230				
1914-S	992,000				
1915	138,000				
1915-D....................	1,170,400				
1915-S	1,604,000				

Half dollar Walking Liberty

	Mintage	Grade	Date purchased	Amount paid	Comments
1916	608,000				
1916-D....................	1,014,400				
1916-S	508,000				
1917	12,292,000				
1917-D Obv. Mint Mark..................	765,400				
1917-D Rev. Mint Mark..................	1,940,000				
1917-S Obv. Mint Mark..................	952,000				
1917-S Rev. Mint Mark	5,554,000				
1918	6,734,058				
1918-D....................	3,853,040				
1918-S	10,282,000				
1919	962,000				
1919-D....................	1,165,000				
1919-S	1,552,000				
1920	6,372,000				
1920-D....................	1,551,000				

Half dollar Walking Liberty (continued)

	Mintage	Grade	Date purchased	Amount paid	Comments
1920-S	4,624,000				
1921	246,000				
1921-D	208,000				
1921-S	548,000				
1923-S	2,178,000				
1927-S	2,392,000				
1928-S	1,940,000				
1929-D	1,001,200				
1929-S	1,902,000				
1933-S	1,786,000				
1934	6,964,000				
1934-D	2,361,400				
1934-S	3,652,000				
1935	9,162,000				
1935-D	3,003,800				
1935-S	3,854,000				
1936	12,614,000				
1936-D	4,252,400				
1936-S	3,884,000				
1936 Proof	3,901				
1937	9,522,000				
1937-D	1,676,000				
1937-S	2,090,000				
1937 Proof	5,728				
1938	4,110,000				
1938-D	491,600				
1938 Proof	8,152				
1939	6,812,000				
1939-D	4,267,800				
1939-S	2,552,000				
1939 Proof	8,808				
1940	9,156,000				
1940-S	4,550,000				
1940 Proof	11,279				
1941	24,192,000				
1941-D	11,248,400				
1941-S	8,098,000				
1941 Proof	15,412				
1942	47,818,000				

Half dollar Walking Liberty (continued)

	Mintage	Grade	Date purchased	Amount paid	Comments
1942-D....................	10,973,800				
1942-D/S................	Incl. above				
1942-S	12,708,000				
1942 Proof	21,120				
1943	53,190,000				
1943-D....................	11,346,000				
1943-S	13,450,000				
1944	28,206,000				
1944-D....................	9,769,000				
1944-S	8,904,000				
1945	31,502,000				
1945-D....................	9,996,800				
1945-S	10,156,000				
1946	12,118,000				
1946-D....................	2,151,000				
1946-S	3,724,000				
1947	4,094,000				
1947-D....................	3,900,600				

Half dollar Franklin

	Mintage	Grade	Date purchased	Amount paid	Comments
1948	3,006,814				
1948-D....................	4,028,600				
1949	5,614,000				
1949-D....................	4,120,600				
1949-S	3,744,000				
1950	7,742,123				

Half dollar Franklin (continued)

	Mintage	Grade	Date purchased	Amount paid	Comments
1950 Proof	51,386				
1950-D	8,031,600				
1951	16,802,102				
1951 Proof	57,500				
1951-D	9,475,200				
1951-S	13,696,000				
1952	21,192,093				
1952 Proof	81,980				
1952-D	25,395,600				
1952-S	5,526,000				
1953	2,668,120				
1953 Proof	128,800				
1953-D	20,900,400				
1953-S	4,148,000				
1954	13,188,203				
1954 Proof	233,350				
1954-D	25,445,580				
1954-S	4,993,400				
1955	2,498,181				
1955 Proof	378,200				
1956	4,032,000				
1956 Proof	669,384				
1957	5,114,000				
1957 Proof	1,247,952				
1957-D	19,966,850				
1958	4,042,000				
1958 Proof	875,652				
1958-D	23,962,412				
1959	6,200,000				
1959 Proof	1,149,291				
1959-D	13,053,750				
1960	6,024,000				
1960 Proof	1,691,602				
1960-D	18,215,812				
1961	8,290,000				
1961 Proof	3,028,244				
1961-D	20,276,442				
1962	9,714,000				
1962 Proof	3,218,019				

Half dollar Franklin (continued)

	Mintage	Grade	Date purchased	Amount paid	Comments
1962-D..................	35,473,281				
1963	22,164,000				
1963 Proof	- 3,075,645				
1963-D..................	67,069,292				

Half dollar Kennedy

	Mintage	Grade	Date purchased	Amount paid	Comments
1964	273,304,004				
1964 Proof	3,950,762				
1964-D..................	156,205,446				
1965	65,879,366				
1966	108,984,932				
1967	295,046,978				
1968-D..................	246,951,930				
1968-S Proof.	3,041,506				
1969-D..................	129,881,800				
1969-S Proof.	2,934,631				
1970-D..................	2,150,000				
1970-S Proof.	2,632,810				
1971	155,164,000				
1971-D..................	302,097,424				
1971-S Proof.	3,220,733				
1972	153,180,000				
1972-D..................	141,890,000				
1972-S Proof.	3,260,996				
1973	64,964,000				
1973-D..................	83,171,400				

Half dollar Kennedy (continued)

	Mintage	Grade	Date purchased	Amount paid	Comments
1973-S Proof.	2,760,339				
1974......................	201,596,000				
1974-D..................	79,066,300				
1974-S Proof.	2,612,568				
1776-1976.............	234,308,000				
1776-1976-D..........	287,565,248				
1776-1976-S..........	6,968,506				
1776-1976-S 40% silver					
Proof...................	3,998,621				
Uncirculated......	4,908,319				
1977......................	43,598,000				
1977-D..................	31,449,106				
1977-S Proof.	3,236,798				
1978......................	14,350,000				
1978-D..................	13,765,799				
1978-S Proof.	3,120,285				
1979......................	68,312,000				
1979-D..................	15,815,422				
1979-S Proof.	3,677,175				
1980-P..................	44,134,000				
1980-D..................	33,456,449				
1980-S Proof.	3,554,806				
1981-P..................	29,544,000				
1981-D..................	27,839,533				
1981-S Proof.	4,063,083				
1982-P..................	10,819,000				
1982-D..................	13,140,102				
1982-S Proof.	3,857,479				
1983-P..................	34,139,000				
1983-D..................	32,472,244				
1983-S Proof.	3,138,765				
1984-P..................	26,029,000				
1984-D..................	26,262,158				
1984-S Proof.	2,748,430				
1985-P..................	18,706,962				
1985-D..................	19,814,034				
1985-S Proof.	3,362,821				
1986-P..................	13,107,633				
1986-D..................	15,366,145				

Half dollar Kennedy (continued)

	Mintage	Grade	Date purchased	Amount paid	Comments
1986-S Proof.........	2,411,180				
1987-P..................	2,834,717				
1987-D..................	2,834,717				
1987-S Proof.........	3,715,041				
1988-P..................	13,626,000				
1988-D..................	12,000,096				
1988-S Proof.........					
1989-P..................					
1989-D..................					
1989-S Proof.........					
1990-P..................					
1990-D..................					
1990-S Proof.........					
1991-P..................					
1991-D..................					
1991-S Proof.........					
1992-P..................					
1992-D..................					
1992-S Proof.........					
1993-P..................					
1993-D..................					
1993-S Proof.........					
1994-P..................					
1994-D..................					
1994-S Proof.........					
1995-P..................					
1995-D..................					
1995-S Proof.........					

$1 silver Flowing Hair

	Mintage	Grade	Date purchased	Amount paid	Comments
1794......................	1,758				
1795 Type of '94...	160,295				

$1 silver Draped Bust, Small Eagle

	Mintage	Grade	Date purchased	Amount paid	Comments
1795......................	42,738				
1796......................	72,920				
1797 9x7 Sm Letters...............	7,776				
1797 9x7 Lg Letters...............	Incl. above				

$1 silver Draped Bust, Small Eagle (continued)

	Mintage	Grade	Date purchased	Amount paid	Comments
1797 10x6...............	Incl. above				
1798 13 St, Small Eagle..................	327,536				
1798 15 St, Small Eagle..................	Incl. above				

$1 silver Draped Bust, Heraldic Eagle

	Mintage	Grade	Date purchased	Amount paid	Comments
1798	Incl. above				
1799	423,515				
1799/98..................	Incl. above				
1799 8x5 Stars........	Incl. above				
1800	220,920				
1801	54,454				
1802/1	41,650				
1802	Incl. above				
1803 Large 3	85,634				
1803 Small 3	Incl. above				

$1 silver Gobrecht

	Mintage	Grade	Date purchased	Amount paid	Comments
1836 circulation....	1,000				
1836 circ., new weight...............	600				
1838......................	(R)				
1839 circulation....	300				

$1 silver Seated Liberty

	Mintage	Grade	Date purchased	Amount paid	Comments
1840 No Motto......	61,005				
1841......................	173,000				
1842......................	184,618				

$1 silver Seated Liberty (continued)

	Mintage	Grade	Date purchased	Amount paid	Comments
1843	165,100				
1844	20,000				
1845	24,500				
1846	110,600				
1846-O	59,000				
1847	140,750				
1848	15,000				
1849	62,600				
1850	7,500				
1850-O	40,000				
1851	1,300				
1852	1,100				
1853	46,110				
1854	33,140				
1855	26,000				
1856	63,500				
1857	94,000				
1858 Proof.	80				
1859	256,500				
1859-O	360,000				
1859-S	20,000				
1860	217,600				
1860-O	515,000				
1861	77,500				
1862	11,540				
1863	27,200				
1864	30,700				
1865	46,500				
1866 Motto	48,900				
1867	47,900				
1868	162,100				
1869	423,700				
1870	415,000				
1870-CC	12,462				
1871	1,073,800				
1871-CC	1,376				
1872	1,105,500				
1872-CC	3,150				
1872-S	9,000				

$1 silver Seated Liberty (continued)

	Mintage	Grade	Date purchased	Amount paid	Comments
1873......................	293,000				
1873-CC................	2,300				
1873-S...................	700				

$1 silver Morgan

	Mintage	Grade	Date purchased	Amount paid	Comments
1878 8 Tail Feathers............	10,508,550				
1878 7TF, rev. '78...	Incl. above				
1878 7TF, rev. '79...	Incl. above				
1878 7/8TF............	Incl. above				
1878-CC................	2,212,000				
1878-S...................	9,774,000				
1879......................	14,806,000				
1879-CC................	756,000				
1879-O..................	2,887,000				
1879-S rev. '78.......	9,110,000				
1879-S rev. '79.......	Incl. above				
1880......................	12,600,000				
1880-CC rev. '78..	591,000				
1880-CC................	Incl. above				
1880-O..................	5,305,000				
1880-S...................	8,900,000				
1881......................	9,163,000				
1881-CC................	296,000				

$1 silver Morgan (continued)

	Mintage	Grade	Date purchased	Amount paid	Comments
1881-O	5,708,000				
1881-S	12,760,000				
1882	11,100,000				
1882-CC	1,133,000				
1882-O	6,090,000				
1882-O/S	Incl. above				
1882-S	9,250,000				
1883	12,290,000				
1883-CC	1,204,000				
1883-O	8,725,000				
1883-S	6,250,000				
1884	14,070,000				
1884-CC	1,136,000				
1884-O	9,730,000				
1884-S	3,200,000				
1885	17,786,837				
1885-CC	228,000				
1885-O	9,185,000				
1885-S	1,497,000				
1886	19,963,000				
1886-O	10,710,000				
1886-S	750,000				
1887/6	20,290,000				
1887	Incl. above				
1887/6-O	11,550,000				
1887-O	Incl. above				
1887-S	1,771,000				
1888	19,183,000				
1888-O	12,150,000				
1888-S	657,000				
1889	21,726,000				
1889-CC	350,000				
1889-O	11,875,000				
1889-S	700,000				
1890	16,802,000				
1890-CC	2,309,041				
1890-O	10,701,000				
1890-S	8,230,373				
1891	8,693,556				

$1 silver Morgan (continued)

	Mintage	Grade	Date purchased	Amount paid	Comments
1891-CC	1,618,000				
1891-O	7,954,529				
1891-S	5,296,000				
1892	1,036,000				
1892-CC	1,352,000				
1892-O	2,744,000				
1892-S	1,200,000				
1893	378,000				
1893-CC	677,000				
1893-O	300,000				
1893-S	100,000				
1894	110,000				
1894-O	1,723,000				
1894-S	1,260,000				
1895	12,000				
1895-O	450,000				
1895-S	400,000				
1896	9,976,000				
1896-O	4,900,000				
1896-S	5,000,000				
1897	2,822,000				
1897-O	4,004,000				
1897-S	5,825,000				
1898	5,884,000				
1898-O	4,440,000				
1898-S	4,102,000				
1899	330,000				
1899-O	12,290,000				
1899-S	2,562,000				
1900	8,830,000				
1900-O	12,590,000				
1900-O/CC	incl. above				
1900-S	3,540,000				
1901	6,962,000				
1901-O	13,320,000				
1901-S	2,284,000				
1902	7,994,000				
1902-O	8,636,000				
1902-S	1,530,000				

$1 silver Morgan (continued)

	Mintage	Grade	Date purchased	Amount paid	Comments
1903	4,652,000				
1903-O	4,450,000				
1903-S	1,241,000				
1904	2,788,000				
1904-O	3,720,000				
1904-S	2,304,000				
1921	44,690,000				
1921-D	20,345,000				
1921-S	21,695,000				

$1 silver Peace

	Mintage	Grade	Date purchased	Amount paid	Comments
1921	1,006,473				
1922	51,737,000				
1922-D	15,063,000				
1922-S	17,475,000				
1923	30,800,000				
1923-D	6,811,000				
1923-S	19,020,000				
1924	11,811,000				
1924-S	1,728,000				
1925	10,198,000				
1925-S	1,610,000				
1926	1,939,000				
1926-D	2,348,700				

$1 silver Peace (continued)

	Mintage	Grade	Date purchased	Amount paid	Comments
1926-S	6,980,000				
1927	848,000				
1927-D	1,268,900				
1927-S	866,000				
1928	360,649				
1928-S	1,632,000				
1934	954,057				
1934-D	1,569,500				
1934-S	1,011,000				
1935	1,576,000				
1935-S	1,964,000				

$1 silver Eisenhower

	Mintage	Grade	Date purchased	Amount paid	Comments
1971	47,799,000				
1971-D	68,587,424				
1971-S Proof.	3,220,733				
1972	75,890,000				
1972-D	92,548,511				
1972-S Proof.	3,260,996				
1973	2,000,056				
1973-D	2,000,000				
1973-S Proof.	2,760,339				
1974	27,366,000				
1974-D	45,517,000				

$1 silver Eisenhower (continued)

	Mintage	Grade	Date purchased	Amount paid	Comments
1974-S Proof.	2,612,568				
1776-1976 Bold Rev Let	117,337,000				
1776-1976 Thin Rev Let	Incl. above				
1776-1976-D Bold Rev Let	103,228,274				
1776-1976-D Thin Rev Let	Incl. above				
1776-1976-S	6,968,506				
1776-1976-S 40% silver					
Proof	3,998,621				
Uncirculated	4,908,319				
1977	12,596,000				
1977-D	32,983,006				
1977-S Proof.	3,236,798				
1978	25,702,000				
1978-D	33,012,890				
1978-S Proof.	3,120,285				

$1 silver Anthony

	Mintage	Grade	Date purchased	Amount paid	Comments
1979-P	360,222,000				
1979-D	288,015,744				
1979-S Filled S	109,576,000				
1979-S Clear S	Incl. above				
1979-S Proof.	3,677,175				
1980-P	27,610,000				
1980-D	41,628,708				
1980-S	20,422,000				

$1 silver Anthony (continued)

	Mintage	Grade	Date purchased	Amount paid	Comments
1980-S Proof.	3,554,806				
1981	3,000,000				
1981-D	3,250,000				
1981-S Filled S	3,492,000				
1981-S Clear S	Incl. above				
1981-S Proof.	4,063,083				

Trade dollar

	Mintage	Grade	Date purchased	Amount paid	Comments
1873	396,635				
1873-CC	124,500				
1873-S	703,000				
1874	987,100				
1874-CC	1,373,200				
1874-S	2,549,000				
1875	218,200				
1875-CC	1,573,700				
1875-S	4,487,000				
1875-S/CC	Incl. above				
1876	455,000				
1876-CC	509,000				
1876-S	5,227,000				
1877	3,039,200				
1877-CC	534,000				
1877-S	9,519,000				

Trade dollar (continued)

	Mintage	Grade	Date purchased	Amount paid	Comments
1878 Proof	900				
1878-CC	97,000				
1878-S	4,162,000				
1879 Proof	1,541				
1880 Proof	1,987				
1881 Proof	960				
1882 Proof	1,097				
1883 Proof	979				
1884 Proof	10				
1885 Proof	5				

$1 gold Coronet

	Mintage	Grade	Date purchased	Amount paid	Comments
1849 Open Wreath, Initial L	688,567				
1849 Closed Wreath	Incl. above				
1849-C Closed Wreath	11,634				
1849-C Open Wreath	Incl. above				
1849-D	21,588				
1849-O	215,000				
1850	481,953				
1850-C	6,966				
1850-D	8,382				
1850-O	14,000				
1851	3,317,671				
1851-C	41,267				
1851-D	9,882				
1851-O	290,000				
1852	2,045,351				
1852-C	9,434				
1852-D	6,360				

$1 gold Coronet (continued)

	Mintage	Grade	Date purchased	Amount paid	Comments
1852-O	140,000				
1853	4,076,051				
1853-C	11,515				
1853-D	6,583				
1853-O	290,000				
1854	736,709				

$1 gold Indian Head, Small Head or Large Head

	Mintage	Grade	Date purchased	Amount paid	Comments
1854 Small Indian Head	902,736				
1854-D	2,935				
1854-S	14,632				
1855	758,269				
1855-C	9,803				
1855-D	1,811				
1855-O	55,000				
1856-S	24,600				
1856 Upright 5, Large Indian Head	1,762,936				
1856 Slant 5	Incl. above				
1856-D	1,460				
1857	774,789				
1857-C	13,280				
1857-D	3,533				
1857-S	10,000				
1858	117,995				
1858-D	3,477				
1858-S	10,000				
1859	168,244				
1859-C	5,235				

$1 gold Indian Head, Large Head (continued)

	Mintage	Grade	Date purchased	Amount paid	Comments
1859-D.................	4,952				
1859-S	15,000				
1860	36,514				
1860-D.................	1,566				
1860-S	13,000				
1861	527,150				
1861-D.............	CSA issue				
1862	1,361,355				
1863	6,200				
1864	5,900				
1865	3,700				
1866	7,100				
1867	5,200				
1868	10,500				
1869	5,900				
1870	6,300				
1870-S	3,000				
1871	3,900				
1872	3,500				
1873 Closed 3.......	125,100				
1873 Open 3........	Incl. above				
1874	198,800				
1875	400				
1876	3,200				
1877	3,900				
1878	3,000				
1879	3,000				
1880	1,600				
1881	7,620				
1882	5,000				
1883	10,800				
1884	5,230				
1885	11,156				
1886	5,000				
1887	7,500				
1888	16,501				
1889	28,950				

$2.50 quarter eagle Capped Bust

	Mintage	Grade	Date purchased	Amount paid	Comments
1796 No Stars..	1,395				
1796 Stars..	Incl. above				
1797..	427				
1798...................	1,094				
1802/1...................	3,035				
1804 13 Stars..	3,327				
1804 14 Stars..	Incl. above				
1805..	1,781				
1806/4...................	1,616				
1806/5...................	Incl. above				
1807..	6,812				

$2.50 quarter eagle Capped Draped Bust

	Mintage	Grade	Date purchased	Amount paid	Comments
1808......................	2,710				

$2.50 quarter eagle Capped Head

	Mintage	Grade	Date purchased	Amount paid	Comments
1821	6,448				
1824/1	2,600				
1825	4,434				
1826	760				
1827	2,800				
1829 Small Planchet	3,403				
1830	4,540				
1831	4,520				
1832	4,400				
1833	4,160				
1834	4,000				

$2.50 quarter eagle Classic Head

	Mintage	Grade	Date purchased	Amount paid	Comments
1834 No Motto	113,370				
1835	131,402				
1836	547,986				
1837	45,080				
1838	47,030				
1838-C	7,908				

$2.50 quarter eagle Classic Head (continued)

	Mintage	Grade	Date purchased	Amount paid	Comments
1839/8	27,021				
1839-C 9 Over 8	18,173				
1839-D 9 Over 8	13,674				
1839-O	17,781				

$2.50 quarter eagle Coronet

	Mintage	Grade	Date purchased	Amount paid	Comments
1840	18,859				
1840-C	12,838				
1840-D	3,532				
1840-O	33,580				
1841 Proof	No record				
1841-C	10,297				
1841-D	4,164				
1842	2,823				
1842-C	6,737				
1842-D	4,643				
1842-O	19,800				
1843	100,546				
1843-C Large Date	26,096				
1843-C Small Date	Incl. above				
1843-D	36,209				
1843-O Small Date	368,002				
1844	6,784				
1844-C	11,622				
1844-D	17,332				
1845	91,051				
1845-D	19,460				
1845-O	4,000				

$2.50 quarter eagle Coronet (continued)

	Mintage	Grade	Date purchased	Amount paid	Comments
1846	21,598				
1846-C	4,808				
1846-D	19,303				
1846-O	62,000				
1847	29,814				
1847-C	23,226				
1847-D	15,784				
1847-O	124,000				
1848	8,886				
1848-C	16,788				
1848-D	13,771				
1849	23,294				
1849-C	10,220				
1849-D	10,945				
1850	252,923				
1850-C	9,148				
1850-D	12,148				
1850-O	84,000				
1851	1,372,748				
1851-C	14,923				
1851-D	11,264				
1851-O	148,000				
1852	1,159,681				
1852-C	9,772				
1852-D	4,078				
1852-O	140,000				
1853	1,404,668				
1853-D	3,178				
1854	596,258				
1854-C	7,295				
1854-D	1,760				
1854-O	153,000				
1854-S	246				
1855	235,480				
1855-C	3,677				
1855-D	1,123				
1856	384,240				
1856-C	7,913				
1856-D	874				

$2.50 quarter eagle Coronet (continued)

	Mintage	Grade	Date purchased	Amount paid	Comments
1856-O	21,100				
1856-S	71,120				
1857	214,130				
1857-D	2,364				
1857-O	34,000				
1857-S	69,200				
1858	47,377				
1858-C	9,056				
1859	39,444				
1859-D	2,244				
1859-S	15,200				
1860 Small Letters & Arrowhead	22,563				
1860-C	7,469				
1860-S	35,600				
1861	1,272,428				
1861-S	24,000				
1862	98,508				
1862/1	Incl. above				
1862-S	8,000				
1863 Proof	30				
1863-S	10,800				
1864	2,824				
1865	1,520				
1865-S	23,376				
1866	3,080				
1866-S	38,960				
1867	3,200				
1867-S	28,000				
1868	3,600				
1868-S	34,000				
1869	4,320				
1869-S	29,500				
1870	4,520				
1870-S	16,000				
1871	5,320				
1871-S	22,000				
1872	3,000				
1872-S	18,000				

$2.50 quarter eagle Coronet (continued)

	Mintage	Grade	Date purchased	Amount paid	Comments
1873 Open 3	178,000				
1873 Closed 3	incl. above				
1873-S	27,000				
1874	3,920				
1875	400				
1875-S	11,600				
1876	4,176				
1876-S	5,000				
1877	1,632				
1877-S	35,400				
1878	286,240				
1878-S	178,000				
1879	88,960				
1879-S	43,500				
1880	2,960				
1881	640				
1882	4,000				
1883	1,920				
1884	1,950				
1885	800				
1886	4,000				
1887	6,160				
1888	16,006				
1889	17,600				
1890	8,720				
1891	10,960				
1892	2,440				
1893	30,000				
1894	4,000				
1895	6,000				
1896	19,070				
1897	29,768				
1898	24,000				
1899	27,200				
1900	67,000				
1901	91,100				
1902	133,540				
1903	201,060				
1904	160,790				

$2.50 quarter eagle Coronet (continued)

	Mintage	Grade	Date purchased	Amount paid	Comments
1905	217,800				
1906	176,330				
1907	336,294				

$2.50 quarter eagle Indian Head

	Mintage	Grade	Date purchased	Amount paid	Comments
1908	564,821				
1909	441,760				
1910	492,000				
1911	704,000				
1911-D	55,680				
1912	616,000				
1913	722,000				
1914	240,000				
1914-D	448,000				
1915	606,000				
1925-D	578,000				
1926	446,000				
1927	388,000				
1928	416,000				
1929	532,000				

$3 gold

	Mintage	Grade	Date purchased	Amount paid	Comments
1854	138,618				
1854-D	1,120				
1854-O	24,000				
1855	50,555				
1855-S	6,600				
1856	26,010				
1856-S	34,500				
1857	20,891				
1857-S	14,000				
1858	2,133				
1859	15,638				
1860	7,036				
1860-S	4,408				
1861	5,959				
1862	5,750				
1863	5,000				
1864	2,630				
1865	1,140				
1866	4,000				
1867	2,600				
1868	4,850				
1869	2,500				
1870	3,500				
1871	1,300				
1872	2,000				
1873 Proof	25(R)				
1874	41,800				
1875 Proof	20(R)				
1876 Proof.	45				
1877	1,468				
1878	82,304				

$3 gold (continued)

	Mintage	Grade	Date purchased	Amount paid	Comments
1879	3,000				
1880	1,000				
1881	500				
1882	1,500				
1883	900				
1884	1,000				
1885	800				
1886	1,000				
1887	6,000				
1888	5,000				
1889	2,300				

$4 gold Stella pattern-only

	Mintage	Grade	Date purchased	Amount paid	Comments
1879 Flowing Hair Proof	pattern				
1879 Coiled Hair Proof	pattern				
1880 Flowing Hair Proof	pattern				
1880 Coiled Hair Proof	pattern				

$5 half eagle Capped Bust,
Small Eagle or Heraldic Eagle

	Mintage	Grade	Date purchased	Amount paid	Comments
1795 Small Eagle.	8,707				
1796/5....................	6,196				
1797 15 Stars.	3,609				
1797 16 Stars.	Incl. above				
1798	24,867				
1795 Heraldic Eagle.................	Incl. above				
1797/5...................	Incl. above				
1797 16 Stars.	Incl. above				
1798 Small 8.	Incl. above				
1798 Large 8, 13 Stars.................	Incl. above				
1798 Large 8, 14 Stars.................	Incl. above				
1799	7,451				
1800	37,628				
1802/1....................	53,176				
1803/2....................	33,506				
1804 Small 8.	30,475				
1804 Sm 8 over Lg 8........................	Incl. above				
1805	33,183				
1806 Pointed 6.	64,093				
1806 Round 6.......	Incl. above				
1807 Right.	32,488				

$5 half eagle Capped Draped Bust

	Mintage	Grade	Date purchased	Amount paid	Comments
1807	51,605				
1808/7	55,578				
1808	Incl. above				
1809/8	33,875				
1810 Small Date, Sm 5.	100,287				
1810 Small Date, Tall 5.	Incl. above				
1810 Large Date, Sm 5.	Incl. above				
1810 Lg Date, Lg 5.	Incl. above				
1811 Small 5.	99,581				
1811 Tall 5.	Incl. above				
1812	58,087				

$5 half eagle Capped Head

	Mintage	Grade	Date purchased	Amount paid	Comments
1813	95,428				
1814/3	15,454				

$5 half eagle Capped Head (continued)

	Mintage	Grade	Date purchased	Amount paid	Comments
1815	635				
1818	48,588				
1819	51,723				
1820 Curved Base 2, Small Letters.	263,806				
1820 Curved Base 2, Large Letters.	Incl. above				
1820 Square Base 2	Incl. above				
1821	34,641				
1822	17,796				
1823	14,485				
1824	17,340				
1825/1	29,060				
1825/4	Incl. above				
1826	18,069				
1827	24,913				
1828/7	28,029				
1828	Incl. above				
1829 Large Planchet.	57,442				
1829 Small Planchet.	Incl. above				
1830 Small 5D.	126,351				
1830 Large 5D.	Incl. above				
1831	140,594				
1832 Curved Base 2, 12 Stars.	157,487				
1832 Square Base 2, 13 Stars.	Incl. above				
1833	193,630				
1834 Plain 4.	50,141				
1834 Crosslet 4.	Incl. above				

$5 half eagle Classic Head

	Mintage	Grade	Date purchased	Amount paid	Comments
1834 Plain 4..........	657,460				
1834 Crosslet 4......	Incl. above				
1835......................	371,534				
1836......................	553,147				
1837......................	207,121				
1838......................	286,588				
1838-C...................	19,145				
1838-D...................	20,583				

$5 half eagle Coronet

	Mintage	Grade	Date purchased	Amount paid	Comments
1839 No Motto......	118,143				
1839-C...................	17,235				
1839-D...................	18,939				
1840......................	137,382				
1840-C...................	19,028				
1840-D...................	22,896				
1840-O...................	38,700				
1841......................	15,833				
1841-C...................	21,511				
1841-D...................	30,495				

$5 half eagle Coronet (continued)

	Mintage	Grade	Date purchased	Amount paid	Comments
1841-O..................	50				
1842 Small Letters	27,578				
1842-C Large Date...................	27,480				
1842-C Small Date...................	Incl. above				
1842-D LD, Lg. Letters..............	59,608				
1842-D SD, Sm. Letters..............	Incl. above				
1842-O.................	16,400				
1843	611,205				
1843-C..................	44,353				
1843-D..................	98,452				
1843-O Small Letters..............	101,075				
1843-O Large Letters..............	Incl. above				
1844	340,330				
1844-C..................	23,631				
1844-D..................	88,982				
1844-O..................	364,600				
1845	417,099				
1845-D..................	90,629				
1845-O..................	41,000				
1846	395,942				
1846-C..................	12,995				
1846-D..................	80,294				
1846-O..................	58,000				
1847	915,981				
1847-C..................	84,151				
1847-D..................	64,405				
1847-O..................	12,000				
1848	260,775				
1848-C..................	64,472				
1848-D..................	47,465				
1849	133,070				
1849-C..................	64,823				
1849-D..................	39,036				
1850	64,491				
1850-C..................	63,591				
1850-D..................	43,984				

$5 half eagle Coronet (continued)

	Mintage	Grade	Date purchased	Amount paid	Comments
1851	377,505				
1851-C	49,176				
1851-D	62,710				
1851-O	41,000				
1852	573,901				
1852-C	72,574				
1852-D	91,584				
1853	305,770				
1853-C	65,571				
1853-D	89,678				
1854	160,675				
1854-C	39,283				
1854-D	56,413				
1854-O	46,000				
1854-S	268				
1855	117,098				
1855-C	39,788				
1855-D	22,432				
1855-O	11,100				
1855-S	61,000				
1856	197,990				
1856-C	28,457				
1856-D	19,786				
1856-O	10,000				
1856-S	105,100				
1857	98,188				
1857-C	31,360				
1857-D	17,046				
1857-O	13,000				
1857-S	87,000				
1858	15,136				
1858-C	38,856				
1858-D	15,362				
1858-S	18,600				
1859	16,814				
1859-C	31,847				
1859-D	10,366				
1859-S	13,220				
1860	19,763				

$5 half eagle Coronet (continued)

	Mintage	Grade	Date purchased	Amount paid	Comments
1860-C	14,813				
1860-D	14,635				
1860-S	21,200				
1861	688,084				
1861-C	6,879				
1861-D	1,597				
1861-S	18,000				
1862	4,430				
1862-S	9,500				
1863	2,442				
1863-S	17,000				
1864	4,220				
1864-S	3,888				
1865	1,270				
1865-S	27,612				
1866 Motto	6,700				
1866-S Motto	34,920				
1866-S No Motto	9,000				
1867	6,870				
1867-S	29,000				
1868	5,700				
1868-S	52,000				
1869	1,760				
1869-S	31,000				
1870	4,000				
1870-CC	7,675				
1870-S	17,000				
1871	3,200				
1871-CC	20,770				
1871-S	25,000				
1872	1,660				
1872-CC	16,980				
1872-S	36,400				
1873 Closed 3	112,480				
1873 Open 3	Incl. above				
1873-CC	7,416				
1873-S	31,000				
1874	3,488				
1874-CC	21,198				

$5 half eagle Coronet (continued)

	Mintage	Grade	Date purchased	Amount paid	Comments
1874-S	16,000				
1875	200				
1875-CC	11,828				
1875-S	9,000				
1876	1,432				
1876-CC	6,887				
1876-S	4,000				
1877	1,132				
1877-CC	8,680				
1877-S	26,700				
1878	131,720				
1878-CC	9,054				
1878-S	144,700				
1879	301,920				
1879-CC	17,281				
1879-S	426,200				
1880	3,166,400				
1880-CC	51,017				
1880-S	1,348,900				
1881	5,708,760				
1881-CC	13,886				
1881-S	969,000				
1882	2,514,520				
1882-CC	82,817				
1882-S	969,000				
1883	233,400				
1883-CC	12,958				
1883-S	83,200				
1884	191,030				
1884-CC	16,402				
1884-S	177,000				
1885	601,440				
1885-S	1,211,500				
1886	388,360				
1886-S	3,268,000				
1887 Proof	87				
1887-S	1,912,000				
1888	18,202				
1888-S	293,900				

$5 half eagle Coronet (continued)

	Mintage	Grade	Date purchased	Amount paid	Comments
1889	7,520				
1890	4,240				
1890-CC	53,800				
1891	61,360				
1891-CC	208,000				
1892	753,480				
1892-CC	82,968				
1892-O	10,000				
1892-S	298,400				
1893	1,528,120				
1893-CC	60,000				
1893-O	110,000				
1893-S	224,000				
1894	957,880				
1894-O	16,600				
1894-S	55,900				
1895	1,345,855				
1895-S	112,000				
1896	58,960				
1896-S	155,400				
1897	867,800				
1897-S	354,000				
1898	633,420				
1898-S	1,397,400				
1899	1,710,630				
1899-S	1,545,000				
1900	1,405,500				
1900-S	329,000				
1901	615,900				
1901-S	3,648,000				
1901/0-S	Incl. above				
1902	172,400				
1902-S	939,000				
1903	226,870				
1903-S	1,855,000				
1904	392,000				
1904-S	97,000				
1905	302,200				
1905-S	880,700				

$5 half eagle Coronet (continued)

	Mintage	Grade	Date purchased	Amount paid	Comments
1906	348,735				
1906-D	320,000				
1906-S	598,000				
1907	626,100				
1907-D	888,000				
1908	421,874				

$5 half eagle Indian Head

	Mintage	Grade	Date purchased	Amount paid	Comments
1908	577,845				
1908-D	148,000				
1908-S	82,000				
1909	627,060				
1909-D	3,423,560				
1909-O	34,200				
1909-S	297,200				
1910	604,000				
1910-D	193,600				
1910-S	770,200				
1911	915,000				
1911-D	72,500				
1911-S	1,416,000				
1912	790,000				
1912-S	392,000				
1913	916,000				
1913-S	408,000				
1914	247,000				
1914-S	247,000				
1914-D	263,000				

$5 half eagle Indian Head (continued)

	Mintage	Grade	Date purchased	Amount paid	Comments
1915	588,000				
1915-S	164,000				
1916-S	240,000				
1929	662,000				

$10 eagle Capped Bust, Small Eagle

	Mintage	Grade	Date purchased	Amount paid	Comments
1795	5,583				
1796	4,146				
1797	14,555				

$10 eagle Capped Bust, Heraldic Eagle

	Mintage	Grade	Date purchased	Amount paid	Comments
1797.....................	Incl. above				
1798/7 9 Stars X 4 Stars.	1,742				
1798/7 7 Stars X 6 Stars.	Incl. above				
1799.......................	37,449				
1800.................,,,,..	5,999				
1801.......................	44,344				
1803.......................	15,017				
1804.......................	3,757				

$10 eagle Coronet

	Mintage	Grade	Date purchased	Amount paid	Comments
1838 No Motto......	7,200				
1839 Old Portrait..	38,248				

$10 eagle Coronet (continued)

	Mintage	Grade	Date purchased	Amount paid	Comments
1839 New Portrait	Incl. above				
1840	47,338				
1841	63,131				
1841-O	2,500				
1842	81,507				
1842-O	27,400				
1843	75,462				
1843-O	175,162				
1844	6,361				
1844-O	118,700				
1845	26,153				
1845-O	47,500				
1846	20,095				
1846-O	81,780				
1847	762,258				
1847-O	571,500				
1848	145,484				
1848-O	35,850				
1849	653,618				
1849-O	23,900				
1850	291,451				
1850 Small Date	Incl. above				
1850-O	57,500				
1851	176,328				
1851-O	263,000				
1852	263,106				
1852-O	18,000				
1853	201,253				
1853/2	Incl. above				
1853-O	51,000				
1854	54,250				
1854-O	52,500				
1854-S	123,826				
1855	121,701				
1855-O	18,000				
1855-S	9,000				
1856	60,490				
1856-O	14,500				
1856-S	68,000				

$10 eagle Coronet (continued)

	Mintage	Grade	Date purchased	Amount paid	Comments
1857	16,606				
1857-O	5,500				
1857-S	26,000				
1858	2,521				
1858-O	20,000				
1858-S	11,800				
1859	16,093				
1859-O	2,300				
1859-S	7,000				
1860	15,055				
1860-O	11,100				
1860-S	5,000				
1861	113,164				
1861-S	15,500				
1862	10,960				
1862-S	12,500				
1863	1,218				
1863-S	10,000				
1864	3,530				
1864-S	2,500				
1865	3,980				
1865-S	16,700				
1865-S inverted 865/186	Incl. above				
1866 Motto	3,750				
1866-S No Motto	8,500				
1866-S Motto	11,500				
1867	3,090				
1867-S	9,000				
1868	10,630				
1868-S	13,500				
1869	1,830				
1869-S	6,430				
1870	3,990				
1870-CC	5,908				
1870-S	8,000				
1871	1,790				
1871-CC	8,085				
1871-S	16,500				

$10 eagle Coronet (continued)

	Mintage	Grade	Date purchased	Amount paid	Comments
1872	1,620				
1872-CC	4,600				
1872-S	17,300				
1873	800				
1873-CC	4,543				
1873-S	12,000				
1874	53,140				
1874-CC	16,767				
1874-S	10,000				
1875	100				
1875-CC	7,715				
1876	687				
1876-CC	4,696				
1876-S	5,000				
1877	797				
1877-CC	3,332				
1877-S	17,000				
1878	73,780				
1878-CC	3,244				
1878-S	26,100				
1879	384,740				
1879-CC	1,762				
1879-O	1,500				
1879-S	224,000				
1880	1,644,840				
1880-CC	11,190				
1880-O	9,200				
1880-S	506,250				
1881	3,877,220				
1881-CC	24,015				
1881-O	8,350				
1881-S	970,000				
1882	2,324,440				
1882-CC	6,764				
1882-O	10,820				
1882-S	132,000				
1883	208,700				
1883-CC	12,000				
1883-O	800				

$10 eagle Coronet (continued)

	Mintage	Grade	Date purchased	Amount paid	Comments
1883-S	38,000				
1884	76,890				
1884-CC	9,925				
1884-S	124,250				
1885	253,462				
1885-S	228,000				
1886	236,100				
1886-S	826,000				
1887	53,600				
1887-S	817,000				
1888	132,924				
1888-O	21,335				
1888-S	648,700				
1889	4,440				
1889-S	425,400				
1890	57,980				
1890-CC	17,500				
1891	91,820				
1891-CC	103,732				
1892	797,480				
1892-CC	40,000				
1892-O	28,688				
1892-S	115,500				
1893	1,840,840				
1893-CC	14,000				
1893-O	17,000				
1893-S	141,350				
1894	2,470,735				
1894-O	107,500				
1894-S	25,000				
1895	567,770				
1895-O	98,000				
1895-S	49,000				
1896	76,270				
1896-S	123,750				
1897	1,000,090				
1897-O	42,500				
1897-S	234,750				
1898	812,130				

$10 eagle Coronet (continued)

	Mintage	Grade	Date purchased	Amount paid	Comments
1898-S	473,600				
1899	1,262,219				
1899-O....................	37,047				
1899-S	841,000				
1900	293,840				
1900-S	81,000				
1901	1,718,740				
1901-O....................	72,041				
1901-S	2,812,750				
1902	82,400				
1902-S	469,500				
1903	125,830				
1903-O....................	112,771				
1903-S	538,000				
1904	161,930				
1904-O....................	108,950				
1905	200,992				
1905-S	369,250				
1906	165,420				
1906-D...................	981,000				
1906-O....................	86,895				
1906-S	457,000				
1907	1,203,899				
1907-D...................	1,030,000				
1907-S	210,500				

$10 eagle Indian Head

	Mintage	Grade	Date purchased	Amount paid	Comments
1907 Wire Rim, Periods	239,406				
1907 Rolled Rim, Periods	Incl. above				
1907 No Periods...	Incl. above				
1908 No Motto	33,500				
1908 Motto	341,370				
1908-D No Motto	210,000				
1908-D Motto	836,500				
1908-S Motto	59,850				
1909	184,789				
1909-D	121,540				
1909-S	292,350				
1910	318,500				
1910-D	2,356,640				
1910-S	811,000				
1911	505,500				
1911-D	30,100				
1911-S	51,000				
1912	405,000				
1912-S	300,000				
1913	442,000				
1913-S	66,000				
1914	151,000				
1914-D	343,500				
1914-S	208,000				
1915	351,000				
1915-S	59,000				
1916-S	138,500				
1920-S	126,500				
1926	1,014,000				

$10 eagle Indian Head (continued)

	Mintage	Grade	Date purchased	Amount paid	Comments
1930-S	96,000				
1932	4,463,000				
1933	312,500				

$20 double eagle Coronet

	Mintage	Grade	Date purchased	Amount paid	Comments
1850 No Motto	1,170,261				
1850-O	141,000				
1851	2,087,155				
1851-O	315,000				
1852	2,053,026				
1852-O	190,000				
1853	1,261,326				
1853/2	Incl. above				
1853-O	71,000				
1854	757,899				
1854-O	3,250				
1854-S	141,468				
1855	364,666				
1855-O	8,000				
1855-S	879,675				
1856	29,878				
1856-O	2,250				
1856-S	1,189,780				
1857	439,375				
1857-O	30,000				

$20 double eagle Coronet (continued)

	Mintage	Grade	Date purchased	Amount paid	Comments
1857-S	970,500				
1858	211,714				
1858-O	35,250				
1858-S	846,710				
1859	43,597				
1859-O	9,100				
1859-S	636,445				
1860	577,611				
1860-O	6,600				
1860-S	544,950				
1861	2,976,387				
1861-O	17,741				
1861-S	768,000				
1862	92,098				
1862-S	854,173				
1863	42,760				
1863-S	966,570				
1864	204,235				
1864-S	973,660				
1865	351,175				
1865-S	1,042,500				
1866 Motto	698,745				
1866-S	722,250				
1866-S Motto	120,000				
1867	251,015				
1867-S	920,750				
1868	98,575				
1868-S	837,500				
1869	175,130				
1869-S	686,750				
1870	155,150				
1870-CC	3,789				
1870-S	982,000				
1871	80,120				
1871-CC	17,387				
1871-S	928,000				
1872	251,850				
1872-CC	26,900				
1872-S	780,000				

$20 double eagle Coronet (continued)

	Mintage	Grade	Date purchased	Amount paid	Comments
1873 Closed 3	1,709,800				
1873 Open 3	Incl. above				
1873-CC	22,410				
1873-S	1,040,600				
1874	366,780				
1874-CC	115,000				
1874-S	1,214,000				
1875	295,720				
1875-CC	111,151				
1875-S	1,230,000				
1876	583,860				
1876-CC	138,441				
1876-S	1,597,000				
1877 TWENTY DOLLARS	397,650				
1877-CC	42,565				
1877-S	1,735,000				
1878	543,625				
1878-CC	13,180				
1878-S	1,739,000				
1879	207,600				
1879-CC	10,708				
1879-O	2,325				
1879-S	1,223,800				
1880	51,420				
1880-S	836,000				
1881	2,220				
1881-S	727,000				
1882	590				
1882-CC	39,140				
1882-S	1,125,000				
1883 Proof	92				
1883-CC	59,962				
1883-S	1,189,000				
1884 Proof	71				
1884-CC	81,139				
1884-S	916,000				
1885	751				
1885-CC	9,450				

$20 double eagle Coronet (continued)

	Mintage	Grade	Date purchased	Amount paid	Comments
1885-S	683,500				
1886	1,000				
1887 Proof	121				
1887-S	283,000				
1888	226,164				
1888-S	859,600				
1889	44,070				
1889-CC	30,945				
1889-S	774,700				
1890	75,940				
1890-CC	91,209				
1890-S	802,750				
1891	1,390				
1891-CC	5,000				
1891-S	1,288,125				
1892	4,430				
1892-CC	27,265				
1892-S	930,150				
1893	344,280				
1893-CC	18,402				
1893-S	996,175				
1894	1,368,940				
1894-S	1,048,550				
1895	1,114,605				
1895-S	1,143,500				
1896	792,535				
1896-S	1,403,925				
1897	1,383,175				
1897-S	1,470,250				
1898	170,395				
1898-S	2,575,175				
1899	1,669,300				
1899-S	2,010,300				
1900	1,874,460				
1900-S	2,459,500				
1901	111,430				
1901-S	1,596,000				
1902	31,140				
1902-S	1,753,625				

$20 double eagle Coronet (continued)

	Mintage	Grade	Date purchased	Amount paid	Comments
1903	287,270				
1903-S	954,000				
1904	6,256,699				
1904-S	5,134,175				
1905	58,919				
1905-S	1,813,000				
1906	69,596				
1906-D	620,250				
1906-S	2,065,750				
1907	1,451,786				
1907-D	842,250				
1907-S	2,165,800				

$20 double eagle Saint-Gaudens

	Mintage	Grade	Date purchased	Amount paid	Comments
1907 High Relief, Roman Numerals, Wire Rim	11,250				
1907 High Relief, Roman Numerals, Flat Rim	Incl. above				
1907	361,667				
1908	4,271,551				
1908 Motto	156,258				
1908-D	663,750				

$20 double eagle Saint-Gaudens (continued)

	Mintage	Grade	Date purchased	Amount paid	Comments
1908-D Motto.......	349,500				
1908-S Motto.........	22,000				
1909/8	161,215				
1909....................	Incl. above				
1909-D.................	52,500				
1909-S....................	2,774,925				
1910....................	482,000				
1910-D.................	429,000				
1910-S..................	2,128,250				
1911....................	197,250				
1911-D.................	846,500				
1911-S..................	775,750				
1912....................	149,750				
1913....................	168,780				
1913-D.................	393,500				
1913-S..................	34,000				
1914....................	95,250				
1914-D.................	453,000				
1914-S..................	1,498,000				
1915....................	152,000				
1915-S..................	567,500				
1916-S..................	796,000				
1920....................	228,250				
1920-S..................	558,000				
1921....................	528,500				
1922....................	1,375,500				
1922-S..................	2,658,000				
1923....................	566,000				
1923-D.................	1,702,250				
1924....................	4,323,500				
1924-D.................	3,049,500				
1924-S..................	2,927,500				
1925....................	2,831,750				
1925-D.................	2,938,500				
1925-S..................	3,776,500				
1926....................	816,750				
1926-D.................	481,000				
1926-S..................	2,041,500				
1927....................	2,946,750				

$20 double eagle Saint-Gaudens (continued)

	Mintage	Grade	Date purchased	Amount paid	Comments
1927-D	180,000				
1927-S	3,107,000				
1928	8,816,000				
1929	1,779,750				
1930-S	74,000				
1931	2,938,250				
1931-D	106,500				
1932	1,101,750				

Commemorative silver, clad

	Mintage	Grade	Date purchased	Amount paid	Comments
1892 Columbian	950,000				
1893 Columbian	1,548,300				
1893 Isabella 25¢	24,191				
1900 Lafayette $1	36,000				
1915 Panama-Pacific	27,134				
1918 Illinois	100,000				
1920 Maine	50,000				
1920 Pilgrim	152,000				
1921 Pilgrim	20,000				
1921 Alabama 2x2	6,000				
1921 Alabama Plain	59,000				
1921 Missouri Plain	15,400				
1921 Missouri 2x4	5,000				
1922 Grant	67,350				
1922 Grant Star	4,250				
1923 Monroe	274,000				
1924 Huguenot	142,000				
1925 Lexington	161,914				
1925 Stone Mountain	1,314,000				
1925 California	86,394				

Commemorative silver, clad (continued)

	Mintage	Grade	Date purchased	Amount paid	Comments
1925 Fort Vancouver........	14,966				
1926 Sesqui.	140,592				
1926 Oregon.........	47,925				
1926-S Oregon......	83,000				
1928 Oregon.........	6,000				
1933-D Oregon....	5,008				
1934-D Oregon....	7,000				
1936 Oregon.........	10,000				
1936-S Oregon......	5,000				
1937-D Oregon....	12,000				
1938 Oregon Set PDS	6,000				
1939 Oregon Set PDS	3,000				
1927 Vermont.......	28,108				
1928 Hawaiian......	10,000				
1934 Boone..........	10,000				
1935 Boone..........	10,000				
1935-D Boone.......	5,000				
1935-S Boone.......	5,000				
1935 Boone Sm. 1934..................	10,000				
1935-D Boone Sm. 1934..................	2,000				
1935-S Boone Sm. 1934..................	2,000				
1936 Boone Sm. 1934..................	12,000				
1936-D Boone Sm. 1934..................	5,000				
1936-S Boone Sm. 1934..................	5,000				
1937 Boone Sm. 1934..................	9,800				
1937-D Boone Sm. 1934..................	2,500				
1937-S Boone Sm. 1934..................	2,500				
1938 Boone Sm. 1934..................	2,095				
1938-D Boone Sm. 1934..................	2,095				
1938-S Boone Sm. 1934..................	2,095				
1934 Maryland.....	25,000				

Commemorative silver, clad (continued)

	Mintage	Grade	Date purchased	Amount paid	Comments
1934 Texas............	61,350				
1935 Texas............	9,988				
1935-D Texas.........	10,000				
1935-S Texas.........	10,000				
1936 Texas............	8,903				
1936-D Texas.........	9,032				
1936-S Texas.........	9,057				
1937 Texas............	6,566				
1937-D Texas.........	6,599				
1937-S Texas.........	6,630				
1938 Texas............	3,775				
1938-D Texas.........	3,770				
1938-S Texas.........	3,808				
1935 Arkansas......	13,000				
1935-D Arkansas...	5,500				
1935-S Arkansas...	5,500				
1936 Arkansas......	9,650				
1936-D Arkansas...	9,650				
1936-S Arkansas...	9,650				
1937 Arkansas......	5,500				
1937-D Arkansas...	5,500				
1937-S Arkansas...	5,500				
1938 Arkansas......	3,150				
1938-D Arkansas...	3,150				
1938-S Arkansas...	3,150				
1939 Arkansas......	2,100				
1939-D Arkansas...	2,100				
1939-S Arkansas...	2,100				
1936 Arkansas (Robinson)	25,000				
1935 Connecticut	25,000				
1935 Hudson	10,000				
1935-S San Diego	70,000				
1936-D San Diego	30,000				
1935 Spanish Trail	10,000				
1936 Albany.........	17,658				
1936 Bridgeport....	25,000				
1936 Cincinnati. ...	5,000				
1936-D Cincinnati.	5,000				

Commemorative silver, clad (continued)

	Mintage	Grade	Date purchased	Amount paid	Comments
1936S Cincinnati.	5,000				
1936 Cleveland....	50,000				
1936 Columbia	9,000				
1936-D Columbia	8,000				
1936-S Columbia	8,000				
1936 Delaware.....	20,978				
1936 Elgin, Ill.	20,000				
1936 Gettysburg...	26,900				
1936 Long Island..	81,773				
1936 Lynchburg...	20,000				
1936 Norfolk..........	16,923				
1936 Rhode Island.................	20,000				
1936-D Rhode Island.................	15,000				
1936-S Rhode Island.................	15,000				
1936 San Francisco..........	71,369				
1936 Wisconsin.....	25,000				
1936 York County	25,000				
1937 Antietam	18,000				
1937 Roanoke	29,000				
1938 New Rochelle	15,251				
1946 Iowa	100,000				
1946 B.T. Washington.......	1,000,546				
1946-D B.T. Washington.......	200,113				
1946-S B.T. Washington.......	500,279				
1947 B.T. Washington.......	100,017				
1947-D B.T. Washington.......	100,017				
1947-S B.T. Washington.......	100,017				
1948 B.T. Washington.......	8,000				
1948-D B.T. Washington.......	8,000				
1948-S B.T. Washington.......	8,000				
1949 B.T. Washington.......	6,000				

Commemorative silver, clad (continued)

	Mintage	Grade	Date purchased	Amount paid	Comments
1949-D B.T. Washington.......	6,000				
1949-S B.T. Washington.......	6,000				
1950 B.T. Washington.......	6,000				
1950-D B.T. Washington.......	6,000				
1950-S B.T. Washington.......	512,091				
1951 B.T. Washington.......	510,082				
1951-D B.T. Washington.......	7,000				
1951-S B.T. Washington.......	7,000				
1951 Wash.-Carver...............	110,018				
1951-D Wash.-Carver...............	10,004				
1951-S Wash.-Carver...............	10,004				
1952 Wash.-Carver...............	2,006,292				
1952-D Wash.-Carver...............	8,006				
1952-S Wash.-Carver...............	8,006				
1953 Wash.-Carver...............	8,003				
1953-D Wash.-Carver...............	8,003				
1953-S Wash.-Carver...............	108,020				
1954 Wash.-Carver...............	12,006				
1954-D Wash.-Carver...............	12,006				
1954-S Wash.-Carver...............	122,024				

George Washington half dollars

	Mintage	Grade	Date purchased	Amount paid	Comments
1982-D..................	2,210,458				
1982-S	4,894,044				

Los Angeles Olympics

	Mintage	Grade	Date purchased	Amount paid	Comments
1983-P Discus Thrower $1........	294,543				
1983-D Discus Thrower $1........	174,014				
1983-S Discus Thrower $1........	174,014				

Commemorative silver, clad (continued)

	Mintage	Grade	Date purchased	Amount paid	Comments
1983-S Proof $1.....	1,577,025				
1984-P Coliseum $1......................	217,954				
1984-D Coliseum $1......................	116,675				
1984-S Coliseum $1......................	116,675				
1984-S Proof $1.....	1,801,210				

Statue of Liberty

	Mintage	Grade	Date purchased	Amount paid	Comments
1986-D Immigrant 50C....................	928,008				
1986-S Immigrant 50C.	6,925,627				
1986-P Ellis Island dollar.................	723,635				
1986-S Ellis Island dollar.................	6,414,638				

Constitution Bicentennial

	Mintage	Grade	Date purchased	Amount paid	Comments
1987-P Constitution dollar.................	451,629				
1987-S Constitution dollar.................	2,747,116				

Olympics

	Mintage	Grade	Date purchased	Amount paid	Comments
1988-P dollar.........					
1988-S dollar.........					

Bicentennial of Congress

	Mintage	Grade	Date purchased	Amount paid	Comments
1989-P half dollar					
1989-S half dollar					
1989-P dollar........					
1989-S dollar					

Eisenhower Centennial

	Mintage	Grade	Date purchased	Amount paid	Comments
1990-P dollar.........					
1990-S dollar					

Commemorative gold

	Mintage	Grade	Date purchased	Amount paid	Comments
1903 Louisiana Purchase Jefferson $1.......	17,375				
1903 Louisiana Purchase Mckinley $1.......	17,375				
1904 Lewis & Clark $1..............	9,997				
1905 Lewis & Clark $1..............	10,000				
1915-S Panama-Pacific $1	15,000				
1915-S Pan-Pac $2.50.................	6,749				
1915-S Pan-Pac $50 Round.	483				
1915-S Pan-Pac $50 Octagonal	645				
1916 McKinley $1	9,977				
1917 McKinley $1	10,000				
1922 Grant Star $1......................	5,000				
1922 Grant Plain $1......................	5,000				
1926 Sesqui-centennial $2.50..................	45,793				
1984-P Torch eagle	33,309				
1984-D Torch eagle	34,533				
1984-S Torch $10	48,551				
1984-W Torch $10	381,085				
1984-W Torch $10 Proof.................	75,886				
1986-W Statue $5	95,248				
1986-W Statue Proof $5.	404,013				
1987-W Constitution $5	214,225				
1987-W Const. Proof $5.	651,659				
1988-W Olympic $5......................					
1988-W Olympic Proof $5..............					
1989-W Congress Bicentennial $5					

Commemorative gold (continued)

	Mintage	Grade	Date purchased	Amount paid	Comments
1989-W Congress Proof $5					

Proof sets

	Mintage	Grade	Date purchased	Amount paid	Comments
* 1936-42 — Coins sold individually; mintage is maximum number of possible sets					
1936......................	3,837				
1937......................	5,542				
1938......................	8,045				
1939......................	8,795				
1940......................	11,246				
1941......................	15,287				
1942......................	21,120				
1950......................	51,386				
1951......................	57,500				
1952......................	81,980				
1953......................	128,800				
1954......................	233,350				
1955......................	378,200				
1956......................	669,384				
1957......................	1,247,952				
1958......................	875,652				
1959......................	1,149,291				
1960......................	1,691,602				
1961......................	3,028,244				
1962......................	3,218,019				
1963......................	3,075,645				
1964......................	3,950,762				
1968......................	3,041,506				
1969......................	2,934,631				
1970......................	2,632,810				

Proof sets (continued)

	Mintage	Grade	Date purchased	Amount paid	Comments
1971	3,220,733				
1972	3,260,996				
1973	2,760,339				
1974	2,612,568				
1975	2,845,450				
1976	4,123,056				
1977	3,236,798				
1978	3,120,285				
1979	3,677,175				
1980	3,554,806				
1981	4,063,083				
1982	3,857,479				
1983	3,138,765				
1984	2,748,430				
1984 Prestige	316,680				
1985	3,362,662				
1986	2,763,504				
1986 Prestige	599,317				
1987	3,792,233				
1987 Prestige	435,495				
1988					
1988 Prestige					
1989					
1990					
1991					
1992					
1993					
1994					
1995					

Uncirculated Mint sets

	Mintage	Grade	Date purchased	Amount paid	Comments
1947	12,600				
1948	17,000				
1949	20,739				
1951	8,654				

Uncirculated Mint sets (continued)

	Mintage	Grade	Date purchased	Amount paid	Comments
1952	11,499				
1953	15,538				
1954	25,599				
1955	49,656				
1956	45,475				
1957	34,324				
1958	50,314				
1959	187,000				
1960	260,485				
1961	223,704				
1962	385,285				
1963	606,612				
1964	1,008,108				
1965 Special Mint Set	2,360,000				
1966 Special Mint Set	2,261,583				
1967 Special Mint Set	1,863,344				
1968	2,105,128				
1969	1,817,392				
1970	2,038,134				
1971	2,193,396				
1972	2,750,000				
1973	1,767,691				
1974	1,975,981				
1975	1,921,488				
1976 40%	1,892,513				
1977	2,006,869				
1978	2,162,609				
1979	2,526,000				
1980	2,815,066				
1981	2,908,145				
1984	1,832,857				
1985	1,710,571				
1986	1,119,957				
1987	2,890,758				
1988					
1989					
1990					

Uncirculated Mint sets (continued)

	Mintage	Grade	Date purchased	Amount paid	Comments
1991					
1992					
1993					
1994					
1995					

American Eagle gold bullion

	Mintage	Grade	Date purchased	Amount paid	Comments
1986 1-ounce Unc.	1,362,650				
1986-W 1-ounce Proof	446,290				
1986 half-ounce Unc.	599,566				
1986 quarter-ounce Unc.....	726,031				
1986 tenth-ounce Unc.	912,609				
1987 1-ounce Unc.	1,045,500				
1987-W 1-ounce Proof	147,498				
1987 half-ounce Unc.	131,255				
1987-P half-ounce Proof	143,398				
1987 quarter-ounce Unc.....	269,255				
1987 tenth-ounce Unc.	580,266				
1988 1-ounce Unc.	465,500				

American Eagle gold bullion (continued)

	Mintage	Grade	Date purchased	Amount paid	Comments
1988-W 1-ounce Proof	87,133				
1988 half-ounce Unc.	45,000				
1988-P half-ounce Proof	76,528				
1988 quarter-ounce Unc. ...	49,000				
1988-P quarter-ounce Proof ..	98,028				
1988 tenth-ounce Unc.	159,500				
1988-P tenth-ounce Proof ..	143,881				
1989 1-ounce Unc. :					
1989-W 1-ounce Proof					
1989 half-ounce Unc.					
1989-P half-ounce Proof					
1989 quarter-ounce Unc. ...					
1989-P quarter-ounce Proof ..					
1989 tenth-ounce Unc.					
1989-P tenth-ounce Proof ..					
1990 1-ounce Unc.					
1990-W 1-ounce Proof					
1990 half-ounce Unc.					
1990-P half-ounce Proof					
1990 quarter-ounce Unc. ...					
1990-P quarter-ounce Proof ..					
1990 tenth-ounce Unc.					
1990-P tenth-ounce Proof ..					
1991 1-ounce Unc.					
1991-W 1-ounce Proof					
1991 half-ounce Unc.					

American Eagle gold bullion (continued)

	Mintage	Grade	Date purchased	Amount paid	Comments
1991-P half-ounce Proof					
1991 quarter-ounce Unc.....					
1991-P quarter-ounce Proof ..					
1991 tenth-ounce Unc.					
1991-P tenth-ounce Proof ..					
1992 1-ounce Unc.					
1992-W 1-ounce Proof					
1992 half-ounce Unc.					
1992-P half-ounce Proof					
1992 quarter-ounce Unc.....					
1992-P quarter-ounce Proof ..					
1992 tenth-ounce Unc.					
1992-P tenth-ounce Proof ..					
1993 1-ounce Unc.					
1993-W 1-ounce Proof					
1993 half-ounce Unc.					
1993-P half-ounce Proof					
1993 quarter-ounce Unc.....					
1993-P quarter-ounce Proof ..					
1993 tenth-ounce Unc.					
1993-P tenth-ounce Proof ..					
1994 1-ounce Unc.					
1994-W 1-ounce Proof					
1994 half-ounce Unc.					
1994-P half-ounce Proof					
1994 quarter-ounce Unc.....					

American Eagle gold bullion (continued)

	Mintage	Grade	Date purchased	Amount paid	Comments
1994-P quarter-ounce Proof ..					
1994 tenth-ounce Unc.					
1994-P tenth-ounce Proof ..					
1995 1-ounce Unc.					
1995-W 1-ounce Proof					
1995 half-ounce Unc.					
1995-P half-ounce Proof					
1995 quarter-ounce Unc. ...					
1995-P quarter-ounce Proof ..					
1995 tenth-ounce Unc.					
1995-P tenth-ounce Proof ..					

American Eagle silver bullion

	Mintage	Grade	Date purchased	Amount paid	Comments
1986 1-ounce Unc....................	5,393,005				
1986-S 1-ounce Proof	1,446,778				
1987 1-ounce Unc....................	11,442,335				

American Eagle silver bullion (continued)

	Mintage	Grade	Date purchased	Amount paid	Comments
1987-S 1-ounce Proof					
1988 1-ounce Unc.					
1988-S 1-ounce Proof					
1989 1-ounce Unc.					
1989-S 1-ounce Proof					
1990 1-ounce Unc.					
1990-S 1-ounce Proof					
1991 1-ounce Unc.					
1991-S 1-ounce proof					
1992 1-ounce Unc.					
1992-S 1-ounce Proof					
1993 1-ounce Unc.					
1993-S 1-ounce Proof					
1994 1-ounce Unc.					
1994-S 1-ounce Proof					
1995 1-ounce Unc.					
1995-S 1-ounce Proof					